A Most Extraordinary Life

A Champion's Journey from Wimbledon to Hollywood, from Aspen to Amazon

Sally Moore Huss

ISBN: 9781945742637

For all those who strive for anything:

Keep Going!

CONTENTS

1 MY FIRST WIMBLEDON

Center Court

Wimbledon was and is considered the world's premier tennis tournament. It has been held at the All England Club in Wimbledon, London since 1877 on grass courts. The inaugural Wimbledon Championship was played in front of 200 spectators, each paying one shilling to watch. The Gentlemen's Singles was the only event held and the winner was awarded a silver cup.

When Novak Djokovic won the 2019 Wimbledon Championship his prize was $2.98 million dollars. And when Simona Halep won the Women's Championship that same year, she earned the same. Isn't that great? Thank you, Billie Jean King and your band of nine who fought for equal rights and prize money! Semi-finalists took in $662,000 each.

I was a semi-finalist once and I have a little bronze medal to prove it... somewhere. All I remember of that day, so long ago, was that I wore a dress I shouldn't have worn and had a forehand that was almost non-existent.

I had not played on the Center Court at Wimbledon before, although I had played at Wimbledon the prior year and had won the Junior Championship. But this was the Ladies' Division, and this was the one that counted. This was the real deal. I was ready, or at least partially ready. I'd spent nine years preparing. Now, it was showtime.

It was a small venue in 1959. The Center Court held a mere 14,000 spectators, a drop in the bucket to what the Center Court now holds. But those 14,000 had 28,000 eyes that all focused on what was happening on that court.

Now that I was there, I would have preferred to have been playing on a back court. The hoopla was milder than what goes on today, but it was still a daunting experience for a young girl from Bakersfield, California. As ready as I appeared to be, I wasn't. I had lost my forehand on the rough and unpredictable grass courts during the Queens Club Championships, just prior to Wimbledon. My favorite stroke had just disappeared and I couldn't seem to find it. This happened to me now and then. But why now? How inconvenient.

As the graceful Brazilian star Maria Bueno and I walked onto the Center Court, I glanced at the surroundings. Linesmen sat in their chairs ready for duty. The umpire looked prepared to oversee the action. The ballboys from the local orphanage were smartly dressed in the colors of the All England Club – green and purple. Then I foolishly glanced at the stadium itself – wall-to-wall people staring down at us, hoping for an exciting battle. I felt absolutely trapped. Having experienced an episode of claustrophobia in a tight crowd before, I knew what to expect. The panic set in. I slowed my pace to calm my nerves. We turned at the designated spot, bowed to the royal box and turned back to find our chairs and put down our belongings. Mine consisted of two Jack Kramer rackets and a purse, the latter holding the essentials – lipstick and some adhesive tape in case a blister should erupt. Then I took off my jacket and looked down at my new tennis dress. I should have played in it previously. You never know what a dress will do. This one seemed to have a mind of its own.

Center Court without a forehand

The dress had a lovely pleated skirt with a huge collar on the front. Both the collar and skirt were trimmed with a pink, floral ribbon. As the wind picked up, that collar flipped up and slapped me in the face. I didn't really pay much attention to it as the play began. I was trying to control my nerves and at the same time locate my absentee forehand. I hoped Maria wouldn't notice my weakness, but of course she did and mercilessly played the forehand side to victory.

It was over in a flash. The 6-2 6-4 score seemed to take no more than ten minutes. All the details of the match became a blur, as did the setting itself. The scuffed-up backcourt where the grass had been worn away, the sound of the umpire's voice, the quiet politeness of the crowd – all were lost on me. I was defeated before the last ball fell into the net.

Hurriedly bowing to the Royal box on my way out

Dumb-founded, I walked off the court and smack into a fuming and furious Teddy Tinling. Waving his arms wildly, he began yelling at me, "Why hadn't you taken a pin and tacked down that collar? Couldn't you understand how embarrassing this would be for me?"

Teddy was the creator of this villainous frock. I was already numb from the loss and now I could feel nothing.

Teddy was the colorful, flamboyant designer of all things glamorous on a tennis court at that time. His creations were frilly and embroidered, hiding little tennis petticoats trimmed with lace beneath pleated or gathered skirts. The fabrics were so fine that any tailor would have been envious.

Teddy on a happier day

To visit this tall, gangly, eccentric, gay blade in his studio was a treat reserved for only the elite players. His tailor shop was small and stuffy, loaded with fabrics, ribbons, and buttons, and zippers... along with his cohort Henry. Henry, a short, ordinary-looking fellow with matted, yellow hair, seemed to be the business partner of the two, while Teddy was the creative genius. Two fittings were required and no change in shape was allowed. The fit was exact; then again, the dress was gorgeous. Everybody loved Teddy, but not me at that moment.

I knew his history – the lace attached to the "panties" of gorgeous Gussie Moran in the 1940s came from Teddy. The gold lame that made up Carol Fagaros' undies in the 1950s was also his creation. Every man offered to polish her golden bloomers, especially when she was in them. Eventually, players like Maria Navratilova, Chris Evert, Evonne Goolagong, and Virginia Wade were all dressed by Teddy. Billie Jean King's Battle of the Sexes attire was designed by him too.

In contrast to the exclusivity of Teddy's stable, anyone could be dressed by Fred Perry. You just went to his warehouse and grabbed anything with a green wreath on it – shirts, skirts, jackets, and warm up suits. The trouble was that you could not be dressed by both. So, if you were lucky enough to be a top player, the House of Tinling was the preferred choice.

Well, of course, I hadn't really been thinking of Teddy or the dress during the match, but mostly about how to hit a forehand. Now I was not only stunned from the defeat, but also from Teddy's tirade. I later found out that his rage stemmed from the fact that Fred Perry, arch rival of Teddy, had been broadcasting our match over the BBC and took the opportunity to point out that the dress, the Teddy Tinling dress, was definitely the cause of my loss. I knew the truth – I had no forehand. I could hardly answer Teddy's attacks. I was too sickened from the loss to respond.

There's always another Wimbledon, I told my teary-eyed self, as I left the grounds in disgrace.

*

To love the way it is, is wise.

To love the way it isn't, is just as wise.

*

Is it possible that life had something else in mind for me? I certainly didn't consider it at that time.

2 THE PERFECT FAMILY

First Trophy

They say that we choose our parents. "They" are those who know. I must have done a good job because I picked the perfect parents… for me.

Is Baby Sally looking into the future?

My father was a great athlete with absolutely no opportunity to develop his athletic ability. Instead, he focused that sporty interest and ability on my brother Bob and me.

My father, future sister-in-law Linda, brother, and mother

My mother was not an athlete, but she was a great cook and a fine homemaker, she could put together a lovely bridge party with hand-made tallies created by her artistic daughter – me. She plied me with art supplies from the moment I could stick my forefinger in a finger-painting set. Private oil painting lessons with a professional artist were given to me at the age of 10 thanks to her. Long, black Prang boxes of crayons tickled my heart, as did little, tin boxes of watercolor paints. I marveled at the colors and what they could do. There were kits to make lariats, others to make necklaces and bracelets out of beads and shells and mounds and mounds of coloring books.

We lived in the wilds of West Covina, California when it was at the edge of a forest of walnut trees. I won my first trophy there. At the age of seven, my father entered me in a soapbox derby race, along with my brother Bob, who was in a different division. We used the same "car." After surveying the hill that I was to travel down, my father nearly withdrew my entry. It was much steeper than any of our practice runs. After some hesitation, he let me proceed. "Let it roll," he instructed, "and when you see me at the bottom of the hill, pull the hand brake." It was the only brake. I hoped I would be strong enough to stop the car and I imagine he did too.

My heart leaped when I was pushed to the top of the hill and saw the crowd on both sides of the street and the distance and the incline I would sail down. I've never been fond of heights. I don't know if that fear started there or later on a chair lift over Aspen Mountain. And where was my father in the crowd? I couldn't see him as I rolled down the hill, but finally spotted him and pulled up the brake. I won a bronze trophy with a car on top. A cleaning woman later placed the trophy on a stool while dusting the mantelpiece in our home, knocked it over, and the car was no longer on top!

I don't remember being upset about this, just as I never truly treasured the trophies I eventually won on a tennis court. Winning them was enough. The truth is that after carting around a box or two of trophies, plates and bowls for years from decades of tennis events, I finally took them to a local church thrift shop in Del Mar and dropped them off. What they were going to do with them I couldn't imagine. But I was never going to have a trophy room or even a case. I was always off to the next adventure.

Strong Will

West Covina was memorable for several things. First, we lived in a home that was owned by a Japanese family who had been sent to an internment camp. It was wartime and the fear of disloyalty by Japanese Americans to the United States resulted in their forced relocation and incarceration of these people into concentration camps. It was considered an ounce of prevention. My father had rented this house from the Saras because he was building our home on the large walnut acreage next door.

While in the Japanese home, I remember testing my will. "I'm going to run away," I announced. I can't remember my gripe. I must have been three or four years old. My clever mother wrapped an apple and a few nuts in a bandana, tied it to a stick and said, "Goodbye." Off I shuffled. I got as far as the end of the driveway. Another time, I claimed, "I'm not going to bed." "Fine." Everyone else turned off the lights and went to bed. That didn't last long either.

I lasted a little longer when I would refuse to eat something on my food plate. I sat there long after everyone else left the table. My father's patience eventually ran out and a little switch to the back of my legs solved that. Again, my mother made accommodations for me. I was only happy eating raw vegetables. As I sat in my highchair, she gave me little bowls of raw peas, raw string beans, slices of raw potato, raw carrots... everything raw, everything so colorful. Clearly, I'd been a vegetarian in my last life and the preference still lingered.

It was a wonderful place to grow up. We had pet rabbits, cats and dogs, and a horse or two. Bob and I swam in the irrigation ditches that were used to water the walnut trees. It was muddy water, but a delight greater than anything I could imagine, except for walking barefooted in the warm dirt on a summer day. "Is it time yet? Can I go barefooted?" I would beg my mother. Again, in her wisdom she would make me wait until the weather was just right before giving permission. It was the "feel" of things that mattered to me. The feel of the soft, dusty earth between my toes was absolutely delicious to me.

We carved forts in the bamboo culvert behind our house. My brother rode bareback on the largest of our horses. Bob looked so small and yet brave on the back of Buck. Bob was especially brave when his finger was caught in the chain of his bicycle and it had to be pushed through the full cycle to be released. I thought I'd die. For some reason I could feel another's pain. I loved him for being so incredibly strong through it all. He had a strong will; so did I.

Who knew our home would be the future city hall and jail of West Covina? It was a large home on a large lot. Who knew that in the future one of my tennis sparring partners at the Los Angeles Tennis Club would be confined to my old bedroom-now-jail-cell for murdering his wife? My mother sent me lurid newspaper accounts of the event when I was playing on the East Coast tennis circuit. It showed Bernie Finch, his paramour, and our home now transformed.

*

Each part of a family adds to the heart

of a family, and the heart of a family is love.

*

I was lucky to have such a fine and supportive family.

3 STARTING TENNIS

First Racket

West Covina was not forever. My father's work sent us off to Bakersfield in central California. That's where our father introduced us to tennis. He bought my brother and me each a tennis racket. Mine was a fine thing, a Dunlop as I remember – wooden, shiny with lacquer and a little red string woven back and forth across the bottom strings. At that time, a string was used to determine who would serve first when the racket was spun. "Rough or smooth?" was the call. That meant which side of the racket had the bumps or no bumps made by the weaving.

In the 1950s there was not that much to do in Bakersfield in the fifties as a youngster. In the summers, we were pre-occupied with staying cool. The temperature would range from 105 degrees to 115 or 120. Houses were equipped with swamp coolers, not air-conditioners, but no matter how high you revved them up, they did not cool the air enough to make you want to do anything energetic. The winters were equally inhospitable when the tule fog rolled in – damp, dark, heavy tule fog, a danger to drive in and a challenge to anyone's lungs. You felt that mold was entering your body with every breath. Actually, it wasn't much different from the smudge we used to inhale in West Covina. There, on cold winter nights metal heating devices called smudge pots, filled with some kind of crude oil, were placed in and around the rows of orange trees, then lighted in an attempt to keep the trees warm and cozy in hopes of saving the crop. In the morning you would wake up with black residue around your nostrils. It was disgusting.

Our cat came to Bakersfield with us, but took off immediately when we opened the car door. No one was thrilled with this move... that was until my father bought us those tennis rackets. What possessed my father to do this, I don't know, but it was a genius move.

My father's natural athleticism came out on the bleached white cement tennis courts at Jastro Park. He had a backhand that you sometimes see in old tennis film footage. It was just a forehand flipped over and hit inside out – every ball hitting on the same side of the racket. Hard on the strings.

He shared what he knew of the game of tennis with my brother and me and his enthusiasm was infectious. It didn't matter if it were tennis or something else, he was enthusiastic about it. And, handsome, wow, he was super manly handsome. Claiming to be a mere 6′2″, he appeared much taller. He exuded a presence of tremendous confidence. I believe that's what made him seem much bigger than he was and he would light up any room he entered. Where did he get that confidence? Nobody gave it to him.

He grew up poor, truly poor, the son of an immigrant family from Switzerland. They lived in a little town called Maricopa. It was all dust and rattlesnakes. It was a suburb of another small town, Taft. Taft may have been big enough to be on a map.

My father could light up a room

My father's father held down a modest job running the pump at a local oil refiner. It left him deaf. The family also homesteaded a bleak piece of land inland from Santa Barbara in the Cuyama Valley.

My grandparents on their fiftieth wedding anniversary

That's where, I think, my father got his strength. He and his mother, my grandmother, would live on this desolate property eight or nine months a year to try to improve it in some way. It was necessary to fulfill the homesteading laws at that time. My grandmother was taking no chances; she had arrived from Switzerland with no birth certificate or passport. The land was bare and had no access to water. My grandfather, who smoked unfiltered Lucky Strike cigarettes for 20 years and only stopped when the U.S. Attorney General noticed that smoking had some connection to lung cancer, had skin that looked like he had been roasted… taught, tight, and ruddy. When he hugged you, it felt like his arms would crack or your ribs would. There was brittleness to his structure, but not to his disposition. He smiled no matter what you said, no doubt because he couldn't hear what you said.

My father and my grandmother took pieces of discarded wood from the Maricopa's dilapidated buildings and built a type of shelter on the homestead. My grandfather brought the wood by horse and wagon, along with food and water once a month, on his only day off. Tucked into the supplies were a scarce number of bullets. They were given to my father who was in charge of the family rifle, and at age seven he became the hunter/provider for the whole family.

With each year's trip back to Maricopa, my grandmother ended up pregnant. Three more sons and a daughter completed the family. My father fed them all. I didn't know any of this about my father's history when I was young, only that he was strong and absolutely reliable, and he loved me unreservedly. In fact, I don't believe this registered consciously; it was an atmosphere that I lived in – safe. Much later, he said that when he played basketball in high school and his team went elsewhere for a game then stopped for a meal, he wouldn't leave the bus; he was afraid he wouldn't eat properly in front of others... in a way that was acceptable. But you wouldn't know this when he was my father. When he was my father, you knew when he walked in a room. Everybody did.

A friend of mine in my college days said of my father, "He makes John Wayne look like a sissy." Probably that's why that friend never became a boyfriend. My father was that impressive.

First Coach

Onto the tennis courts we would go with our father. He hit balls to us until it was dark, then plunked a quarter into a box on a pole to turn on the lights. At some point it became obvious that we needed proper instruction. A wonderful man named Lake Lovelace began giving us tennis lessons there at Jastro Park. Lake was one of those people who seemed always to have been old. It was probably because he was surprisingly wise and had such a kind, soft face. His nature was equally gentle. I have to tell you that you can meet the nicest people in the world on a tennis court, whether it's someone to give you a lesson or hit a few balls with you. Lake Lovelace was one of them.

Lake loomed large in the tennis world in Bakersfield. He was the only one who really knew much about the game. He taught from a camp chair planted at the net. Popping balls to my brother and me, he would tell us what to do. He couldn't show us because he was disabled. His legs had been badly damaged in a car accident long before.

Under bright lights on a summer's evening or on a lazy Sunday afternoon at Jastro Park the courts did not go idle. You see, many African-Americans played tennis there. In those early days in Bakersfield, there was little interaction between the African-American community and the whites. The African-Americans generally worked in the various service industries or in the fields picking cotton. It was quite a separated structure. This was the 1950s. The separation was not by law, but rather somehow by tradition – yet not on the tennis court. There, we were color-blind. We played with each other for years; even long after Bakersfield had its own proper tennis club. These delightful people filled the courts with laughter, friendly jibs, unconventional strokes, good sportsmanship, and always had a picnic under the pepper trees after the tennis. It seems to me, as I look back, that those who have little appreciate everything. That's what they did. I didn't think about that then, I just enjoyed the sunny, warm days and evenings with tennis friends. They usually brought along a bottle or two of soda pop, which they generously shared. Bottled sodas were rare. Most everyone drank homemade lemonade.

A few years later, a group of the fine folks at the park, including my father, gathered enough funds to build Lake his own tennis club – the Bakersfield Racquet Club, it was called. It was his dream.

Among the highlights of my early days at the Racquet Club were the tournaments. We had turkey tournaments, where practically everyone who could hit the ball over the net won a turkey. There were also bisque tournaments that consisted of a very elaborate system of ranking doubles teams and allotting an appropriate number of bisques or tokens per team to even the play. (The bisques represented points and if you had an add, you could just buy the game with one of your bisques, or use them all to buy a game, if you had four.) These were all family events, fun events, nothing serious. Lake continued giving my brother and me tennis lessons and my father kept hitting us practice balls.

First Goal

Of course, like all kids, we were going to school. Mine was next door to the tennis club, Franklin Elementary. Occasionally my father and Lake would make me take a day off from tennis. On those days, I would look out the school bus window at the tennis courts on my way home and wonder if I would still be able to hit a ball in the court the next day. I seemed to have the idea that tennis could get away from me if I weren't playing it all the time. I was already developing my identity as a tennis player at this young age. No other kids in my class seemed to be working on something so intensely. But then no one had a father like mine.

The principal of Franklin Elementary was the most stern and scary woman I've ever seen and whose name I've repressed. She had a ritual of giving our class spelling tests each week... herself. We had to write with a stick pen and ink from a bottle that sat on top of our desks. Not only did we have to be correct in the spelling, we also had to manage writing with this cumbersome tool. Scratching out words with that pen, with a point would catch on the paper, splattering the ink around the rest of the page, was a struggle. I didn't appreciate the beauty of this exercise until much later. It seemed, at that time, to be pointless and unnecessary and even resulted in a tattoo when the pen accidentally pricked my thumb. While pointing to the tattoo, a doctor later asked me if I belonged to a secret society. Hardly.

Beginning tennis with a beginning backhand

Balls, balls and yet more balls. With each basket of balls hit I was getting better. The basket was filled and emptied again and again. Hundreds of balls a day were hit, thousands perhaps. Effort, that's what it took to get better. It was at this point that my father and I had a serious talk about tennis. We had stopped at a wooden bench after our practice session. The sky was hazy and colorless, the way it usually was during those foggy winter days in Bakersfield. My father's demeanor was thoughtful. Putting one foot up on the bench, he looked down at me, "How good would you like to be?" he asked. The thought had never occurred to me. I didn't have great dreams. I was just going along with the program. "Why not be the best you can be? Why not be a champion?" he asked. Hmmm.

We had travelled to Los Angeles with Lake and a few other club members to watch real champions give exhibitions. They were champions like Pancho Gonzales, Jack Kramer, Pancho Segura and Tony Trabert. I didn't know anyone could hit a tennis ball so hard and in so many different ways as these players could. I was thoroughly impressed, but I'd never thought about being a champion myself.

Now I did, "Okay," I said. I was ten.

*

Nothing stands in the way of a person with a goal

and nothing stands in the way of a person without one.

*

Instantly I had one.

4 SERIOUS TENNIS

What Was a Champion?

To be a champion in those days was different than being a champion today. It was very simple: all you had to do was win Wimbledon. A player could win the French, the Australian or the U.S. Championship at Forest Hills, or all three and still not be considered "The Champion," unless he or she won Wimbledon. There were no points to accrue, no money to be won or material gain to be had. These were the days before the "open" era. People played for the thrill of competing and the glory of winning.

Where did my father get this idea of making me a champion? He had come from such a humble background. It is a wonder that anyone in that family ever thought of striving for greatness in anything – or maybe it was because of that. I remember sitting next to him as he listened to the calls of the horse races at Santa Anita on the radio. Or, sharing a bowl of popcorn while hearing the triumphs of the Brooklyn Dodgers game by game. He definitely had sporting blood.

Years later he told me that during one of my early

tennis lessons Lake had pointed to me and said, "There's your champion." My father took it seriously. Yep, he had tested me even earlier when he threw me in the water at Newport Beach. I was eight and had to swim across the bay. He watched from a small rowboat next to me, but still I was doing the dog paddling in an effort to swim. Then there was that soapbox derby race where I won a trophy. I liked that.

Trophies were good, although later they seem to lose their luster. They made you realize that you'd accomplished something, I suppose. Parents sometimes thought differently, I figured. One year some adults put on a pet show for all the neighborhood kids. Everybody brought what they had – dog, cat, rat, snake, hamster, rabbit, and so on. When the ribbons were awarded, every child's animal won a ribbon... for something. Even my old gray cat that had finally graced us with her return, won a ribbon for her "coat." This was not a real contest. Any kid could see that. I wanted to "win" something that really meant something!

There was a thrill to winning. Perhaps that's the danger in competition: when the "winning" takes precedence over the activity. It's the effort in sports that leads to winning. In tennis, once the focus goes to the result, wishing and wanting a particular outcome, the attention to the ball disappears. Without that focus on the ball, the results are less than desirable. It's a matter of making an effort without asking for anything in return. I only learned this later, but would have benefitted by this attitude if I had had it when I was a young player.

My father and I were making a pact that we would work together to make me a champion. As I recall, there was no resistance on my part. I was just a little girl doing what I was told to do, what needed to be done. I was malleable and, in this way, I was all in. My father directed the way. He was in charge.

The next step in this great adventure was to find a better, more experienced coach.

A Better Coach

You could not find a better coach than George Toley. Anyone who knew him would agree. He was intelligent, knowledgeable, accomplished, principled and dedicated. Lake and my father found him. There were only a handful of coaches in the Southern California area. George was considered the best. He held the premier position as the Director of Tennis at the renowned Los Angeles Tennis Club.

The best coach – George Toley

My heart would go pitter-patter when I'd enter this

bastion of tennis, even for just a tennis lesson. The front room, an enormous airy space with a high ceiling, tall windows, and elegant cream-colored silk drapes, had large framed photos of past tennis champions hanging on the walls. Champions like Bill Tilden, Ellsworth Vines, Helen Wills, May Sutton Bundy, Bobby Riggs, and Alice Marble looked down on me as I walked through the room toward the courts. It is where all the greats of the past had played and some still did. Players like Jack Kramer, Maureen Connelly, Louise Brough, Don Budge, Pancho Gonzales, and Ted Schroeder could be seen on a practice court now and then. It was impressive.

It was also the home of the Southern California Tennis Association, housed in a small set of offices just to the right off of the club's lunch room. That association was ruled by the infamous Perry T. Jones, a man of small stature who wheeled big power. Shaped and dressed in black and white like a penguin, Mr. Jones sat in his office in front of impressive glass cases filled with silver trophies and platters, and the real Davis Cup. Mr. Jones was in charge of which American players were allowed to play the tournaments in Europe and on the east coast. He didn't like Jews or Mexicans (i.e., Pancho Gonzales), but he did like me. I was polite and kept my tennis shoes white. Most tennis shoes were made of canvas. The only way to clean them was to use a type of shoe paint – and I could paint.

The biggest event of the year at that club was the star-studded Pacific Southwest Tournament with as many stars in the audience as on the courts. Jean Simons, Stewart Granger, Dinah Shore, Robert Stack, Kirk Douglas, Robert Wagner and more filled the stands and boxes.

Outside the L.A. Tennis Club in a homemade tennis dress

Besides this top teaching position at the LATC, George was the head tennis coach of the men's team at the University of Southern California, and on the side, he taught tennis to the privileged students at the private Marlborough Girls' School, near the exclusive residential area of Hancock Park. How exclusive was it? The Archbishop of Los Angeles had a home there and when the popular African-American singer Nat King Cole bought a home within those gates, the Ku Klux Klan, still active in Los Angeles then, placed a burning cross on his front lawn. The property owners' association told Cole they did not want any undesirables moving into the neighborhood. Cole responded, "Neither do I. And if I see any undesirables coming in here, I'll be the first to complain!" None of Cole's children went to Marlborough, but if they had, George would have welcomed them.

George was a tall man, like my father, but thinner with an overly tanned, weathered face, and a warm smile that was somewhat crooked due to some complicated dental work that had gone awry. He was a superior tactician. He knew strokes. He knew strategy and he knew grips. Mine had to go. I had a western grip on my forehand that had my hand turned well under the racket handle. Eastern grips were the thing at that time with the hand and racket face in alignment. Oh my, this was a big challenge for me as a young player. It was hard for me to change something that I was used to. It still is, no matter what it is. The new grip was awkward and strange at first. However, with my father's determination and patience, we did it. The funny thing is that now everyone is taught to use a western grip, which lofts the ball well clear of the net, allowing it to fall inside the baseline with tremendous spin, but not then. Flat, hard balls were what we learned to hit. George knew best. I was in George's hands, literally.

If I didn't get the grip right or a motion right, George would come around the net and with his big, broad hands take my hand or my arm and carry it through the correct motion. It was awkward, but it worked. I felt what he meant and could duplicate it. To get someone to feel a motion was so much better than just talking about it. I used this technique much later myself when I taught tennis. Words can be so limiting. It is the feeling that gives us the best understanding of something. Feeling makes it stick, makes it memorable.

Everyone played with wooden rackets, not anything you'd put a brace on to keep from warping like the players did in the 1930s and 1940s. Those braces were cumbersome contraptions, squarish in shape with screws to tighten and hold the racket head in form. The wooden rackets we used did not require a brace. It's not that we wanted wooden rackets, that was all that existed, and a limited variety at that. The Jack Kramer racket was my racket of choice as I advanced in the game. Yes, the Kramer for rackets and Converse or Purcell for shoes. We didn't have many choices for anything. Tennis dresses were made of something called sharkskin. It was a beautiful material that hung on the body gracefully. It was cream-colored, light and flexible, giving you room to move freely. You might say it was danceable. I had one or two in my closet. Sharkskin also required serious ironing. My mother was in charge of that. Other than the two styles of sharkskin dresses you could find on a rack, handmade dresses were the other option. A pair of Converse sneakers cost $15. I don't remember if there were any tennis bags, those big lumpy things that nearly every player walks on the court with today. I still don't use a tennis bag, probably from habit.

George had a small tennis shop at the L.A. Tennis Club where he sold rackets, tennis clothes and shoes, tennis balls, and where he strung rackets. He was a master at "patching" a broken string. No one bothers to do that anymore. Everyone just rips out a set of strings if one string breaks and has the whole racket restrung. But then, it was an art to be able to patch a racket and still maintain tension in the string job. George knew how to do it. The secret was not to hit another ball after a string had broken. This way he could recapture the tension. If you did, he couldn't. After he'd fix it, he'd slap on a brushstroke of shellac on each side of the strings to seal them and complete the job. I can still smell that shellac now. A new set of nylon strings cost about $8 and a set of gut $12.

George was a man who had everything in its place. There was nothing messy about him or his shop or his home.

Everything was orderly and his spaces were as efficient as he was. He had a small workshop behind one of the back courts at the club where he housed his ball machines. These were dangerous machines that could break your arm if you got in the way of their actions. He could keep these antiquated contraptions in working order with a few tweaks of screwdriver or wrench. If he didn't have what he needed, he could find the solution in a hardware store. To see him walk down the aisles of a hardware store with eyes lit up you might have thought he was in Tiffany's. He loved to tinker.

A 1955 red Ford Thunderbird convertible, the hottest car ever built, was George's pride and joy. He kept it in pristine condition. That was George: master of machines and all that was around him, including his pupils. That's why his teams at USC won 10 NCAA championships while he was their coach, and over the years his pupils won 429 national and international titles, which included Stan Smith's 49, Raul Ramirez's 30, Dennis Ralston's 24, and my 21.

*

A good coach believes in the greatness of players

and then coaches it out of them.

*

George was such a coach. Again, I was lucky.

5 CENTER OF ATTENTION

Our Family Focus

Once we had picked George to be my coach, our family focused on my tennis, or so it seemed to me. Was this right? It's hard to say. It's what we did. I had no particular say in the matter. I'd made a commitment to my father. As usual, I didn't really think about it. I was being groomed to be a tennis champion. That's all. This was our goal and it included everybody. The objective was for me to be that champion and not just one of the players. Anyone could fill a draw, but not me. That was not our goal. My father set the vision and he held the reins. I did the work on the court, and it was work perfecting a stroke or mastering a shot, ball by ball. Then again, there was satisfaction in having accomplished something. My mother's role in all this was to feed me well and make sure that my tennis clothes were washed and ironed. Gratitude was not a part of my consciousness as a young person. Everyone did what was expected and I accepted it all as normal.

The commitment my father made was, of course, enormous. It was not just the hours on the tennis court that he spent with me feeding me zillions of balls. There was the time, effort and money he used driving the 100 plus miles from Bakersfield to Los Angeles for a lesson every weekend and sometimes twice a weekend. It took an hour and 45 minutes each way. Not once do I remember saying, "Thank you."

Very shortly, our family vacations were centered on my tournament schedule. I accepted it all without recognizing that there were sacrifices involved. Everyone in the family gave up time and energy to help me accomplish this dream. Was it my dream? Was it my father's? Was it ours? I certainly would never have embarked on it alone. I didn't have that kind of drive or strength. Who gave up what for this effort?

My mother gave up time with her husband, and my brother with his father as my father spent most of his after-hours' time working with me. My mother was always in the background, it seemed. She was a lovely woman and was full of intelligence and goodness. She was from a more upper-class family than my father and had been a schoolteacher when they met. Such a cook! That was probably one of her most outstanding talents. She could make any food better by what she did to it and could fix a stunning flower arrangement to go along with the meal. Her eyes were soft and her true character, basic goodness, was hidden behind them. There was a melancholy in her that she revealed only on Sundays when I would accompany her to church. This sadness that fell over her there affected me in a way that made me not want to attend – a deep sorrow was present within her that was never explained. I believe I inherited that sorrow, held just below the surface, and have transformed it through the years with joy. I have been told that we come into this life with the key to a particular negative characteristic that runs in a family or a member of a family. Perhaps that's what I was here to do for her.

Where my brother fell in this mix, I don't remember. I was too self-absorbed to notice. He never made this loss of our father's attention to him known to me. That's one of the great drawbacks in creating a champion or being a champion... this self-centeredness, self-importance, and obsession with accomplishment. Where is the balance? Where was the balance in my case?

It's a real conundrum. It takes enormous effort and focus to do something outstanding and at the same time, something else is lost along the way. Could it be the opportunity to simply stop and smell the roses?

Yes, accomplishments have their place but they're not everything. They're not the only things. Even today I find myself working beyond the point of "enough." Would hitting another basket of serves when I was a child have helped? Would another drawing for another greeting card have made a difference when I was creating a line of cards for American Greetings? Would writing another children's book help more mothers discover my already extensive line of books? It's a trait that seems to be built into a thoroughbred: more must be better. With this kind of thinking, a person can't just quit and say I've done enough for now. It's not in their DNA. So, a person should be forewarned and a sense of proportion should be taken into account when creating a champion or developing a champion's mentality. Effort should be made with balance in mind. Inner harmony is the goal, as it brings out the best in every situation, and without it an ingrained fear can take over. If I don't do this, what could happen? The idea is to get rid of fear, on or off the tennis court, the golf course, the football field, the basketball court, or elsewhere. To perform fearlessly in whatever the endeavor is the goal, higher even than winning. Winning comes on its own anyway. As a friend of mine would say, "Results are none of our business." Our business is effort. The trick is to balance the effort. I think effort with love makes the perfect balance. I'm still struggling with it, however now and then I do stop and smell the roses, or the ocean, or the pine trees.

What About Art?

It took a lot of gallivanting of the whole family to get me where I needed to go. You may not have heard of it, but once there was a car called a Studebaker. It was a long, odd thing with peculiar angles and a porpoise's nose for a front grill. We had one, thanks to the company my father worked for. It was a trusty vehicle that would carry us over the dreaded two-lane Ridge Route highway from Bakersfield to L.A. every weekend for my tennis lessons. The whole family went along. During the week, my father and I worked on everything I had been taught, and then returned again for more instruction. Back and forth we would drive collecting information and honing skills. I don't mean to say that it was all work. We would explore different restaurants on these trips – Van de Kamp's or Du Par's, usually nothing fancy. I was happy. I was always happy spending time with my father; his positive nature brightened anyone in his presence... but you certainly didn't want to be on the wrong side of him.

It was on one of these trips that my mother approached the subject of art. "What about her art?" She asked.

Art had been what I did during any spare moment and

in school. My dear mother, from my earliest memories of her, was the supplier and supporter of my interest in art. The oil painting lessons she arranged for me came at the same time that I started tennis. I loved it. I loved the smell of the turpentine, the linseed oil, and the oil paints themselves. It was a magical thing to be able to take an empty canvas and with a brush and paint create something that resembled something.

First oil painting, age 10

My teachers in my early grammar school days gave me extra help when it came to art projects. One bought me a set of over-sized, thick crayons that she cut into various lengths and showed me how to move them in different ways to create unusual strokes on a page. Art was something that I loved to do, but that was all. I never considered a career in art. I was going to be a tennis champion.

"What about art?" my father laughed. Art was nothing to him compared to tennis. He jokingly suggested that we use one of my creations on the floor of the garage to collect the oil drippings under our car. It didn't hurt my feelings. I knew he was joking or at least half joking. No, my father was the dominant one. It was tennis only. In fact, he was so dominant that I don't remember ever opposing him on anything, certainly not on this. My mother was similarly silent.

*

It takes effort to get anywhere or to accomplish anything.

Effort is everything.

*

From a young age I learned to put in the effort.

6 A BETTER LIFE

Learning About the Rich

As I started to play tournaments, I often spent weekends in Los Angeles. As the tennis instructor at the private Marlborough Girls School, George would occasionally house me for a long weekend at one of the Marlborough girls' homes. These were fine homes with marble, wood and leather, books and paintings, linen and silver. It gave me a glimpse into how the affluent and truly wealthy lived. Mostly, I was observant. No one sat me down and told me how to act. I kept my eyes open and followed their example. One of the girls did whisper to me, "Don't pick the bread up when you butter it, leave it on the plate... and only a small piece at a time." To be correct was my wish. I learned the manners used in these households: how to sip soup without slurping, how to hold a knife, which fork to use with which course, how to dress for dinner, and even how to write a thank you note to my hostess when I returned home. I loved learning about this more sophisticated lifestyle. I was beginning to feel right at home when the butler would enter the library and announce, "Dinner is served."

I was envious of the Marlborough girls' demeanor, of their tasteful clothes with their initials embroidered on their sweaters – and also their hairdos. They had been to hair salons and had professionals cut and groom their hair. My mother cut mine and she wasn't trained. I'm not sure it was "envy"; it might have been a kind of admiration that I had for these girls, or their tastes. They all looked like the popular actress of the time, Grace Kelly. It was an aesthetic quality about them that was more refined than what I was used to. I secretly coveted it. I could see the difference. They seemed to me to be a cut above. Now and then, I would daydream of going to school at Marlborough and being their equal, whatever that meant. The truth is these girls never looked down on me. Perhaps ironically, they looked up to me because of my tennis ability.

I wasn't resentful in any way of my own circumstances. If I thought about it, I appreciated what I had – I just had a hunger for more.

Being a child of the 1950s, I was encouraged to improve my status in life. Every generation, it was assumed, would do better than their parents. This meant more money, a finer home, a better education, and more advantages in every way, including memberships to clubs. At that time there were not a lot of tennis clubs and if they existed, they existed for the wealthy. Tennis was generally considered an upper-class sport. Now it is quite different, anyone can excel and compete with less concern for what courts they learned on. But in the 1950s, tennis was still a sport for the privileged.

I was definitely directed upwards. I liked the prettier, finer things and the elegance that I saw around me when I visited these homes. Modest surroundings and ordinary tastes were my experience. Tennis afforded me the opportunity to explore a different style of living, to learn what it meant to be "cultured" and then learn to be comfortable in "polite society" ... a society filled with what I thought was "quality."

Little did I realize then that the home I was born into was of the highest quality of all that really matters. My parents were loving, generous and ethical. When it was time to have our parents pick us up at the movie theater, other kids would put a dime in the phone, let it ring once, hang up and the dime would return. That would be the signal to be picked up. Not my parents. It wasn't right. Put in the dime, make the call and wait for someone to answer. The dime belonged to the phone company.

This more cultured education that I was acquiring in these girls' homes came in handy when later I travelled to the east coast to play tournaments. All the players were housed in the finest homes and estates of the members of the clubs where the championships were held – the Merion Cricket Club in Main Line Philadelphia, the Orange Lawn Tennis Club in New Jersey, Forest Hills in New York, Essex Lawn Tennis Club in Manchester, Massachusetts, and the Longwood Club in Boston. This was long before money was introduced to the sport. So, no one stayed in hotels. Only a few of the men players received any money for their expenses and that was usually slipped to them "under the table." No one talked about it, but we knew it was going on. The rest of us had to fund our travels ourselves or from donations from our local clubs or tennis associations. The Southern California Tennis Association was very generous with me, as was the Bakersfield Racquet Club. I hope I made them proud.

I suppose, my father and I worked for this "better life" unconsciously through the avenue of tennis. I wasn't aware of it, although he might have been. Truly, it was a side product and not the goal. As always, the goal was to become champion.

A determined junior

*

Your worth is invaluable.

Your knowing it is priceless.

*

A young person's self-worth can easily get mixed up with accomplishments. I'm sure mine did.

7 REAL COMPETITION

Competing in the Juniors

Once I could hit the ball in the court consistently, I began playing junior tennis tournaments. My brother played too, although his ability to change physical movements and learn quickly was limited. He worked at his game as I worked on mine with our father's help. He started a bit too late to reach great heights in the sport. Yet he played and enjoyed tennis his whole life.

My brother Bob was an amazing person, always stable and balanced, even as a kid. Nothing rattled him much. If family friends made a surprise visit to our home in an evening and he was tired, he'd go to bed. By contrast, I never wanted to miss a party. He was our mother's son, closer to her nature than to our father's. Of course, as young kids we fought fiercely but then would side with each other when other kids challenged us from the outside. He protected me.

Bob took wins and losses easily – not me. He had other interests besides tennis and did well in school. Eventually, he floated away from competitive tennis.

At that time our mother was our chauffeur to these

events through the summers… Santa Barbara, Ventura, San Diego, Santa Monica, Coronado and La Jolla. La Jolla touched my heart with its beautiful beaches and charming village. I vowed that I would live there one day and I did. It is amazing how you can plant a seed, a wish, or a goal strongly and eventually, if not changed, it will come true.

During this time, my father stayed home and worked. I did what I was told to do, "Go out, hit hard and win." I was given no other instructions or strategy. Thinking was not my forte. No one asked me to think and I didn't think on my own.

In the beginning, I lost. Time and again like every kid who lost, I was disappointed and full of tears. A lump in my throat would start to well up as the inevitable defeat was in the making. I hated to lose. I'm not sure why. No one got mad or yelled at me. Perhaps it was just plain competitiveness on my part, to be better than my competitor – or was it having a goal and not reaching it that was so disturbing? Winning was what I was sent out to do. That's what I wanted.

Competition can put a terrible strain on a young person. Coaches and parents want something. They want results for their efforts, for their investment, even if it is not spoken. How can it be done in a way that allows a young person to perform at their best, free of the fear and anxiety associated with letting themselves and others down? When demands or caveats are present in an activity, even subconsciously, a tightening and constricting occurs in the body, preventing it from performing at its peak. Better for a player to have inner harmony as the goal, make the effort, and be accepting of whatever happens. It is a way of playing freely, which releases enormous energy. It is a Zen way of approaching competition. It wasn't until years later that I found this to be true.

Finally, I reached a point in my development that I began winning. In tournaments that I had lost in the prior year, I now won – the Dudley Cup in Santa Monica, the tournaments in Ventura and Burlingame. I was on the brink of winning the tournament in La Jolla too when the girl I was playing in the finals spoke to me during the break after we had split sets. "My father is going to kill me if I lose this match," she said. "Could you let me win?"

Sweet revenge and a proud father

Basically a "pleaser" and not prone to thinking, I dumped the match. My father couldn't figure it out and I didn't say anything. She was a friend. When I finally understood that I'd been had, I beat that same girl in the finals the following week at Coronado – and without an ounce of regret.

I was determined and kept at it. In one tournament in Griffith Park, near Burbank, George came out to watch me play. The smog was so thick that it was nearly impossible to breathe and my chest hurt. People in the L.A. area today don't know or remember how bad the air was before unleaded gas. It was awful. The fumes from cars would collect and just sit in the bowl around the Burbank-Van Nuys-Pasadena area. When my opponent and I split sets and I came off the court for a break, George wanted me to default. No, I kept going. I can't even remember whether I won that match or not. I was certainly determined to play it out. I had a definite sense of completion: if you started something, you should see it through.

On our family vacation one year, we took the train to Chicago. There was a national tournament being held at Chicago's Beverly Hills Tennis Club on a red clay surface. In preparing me for the clay, George had arranged for me to practice on the only clay court in California at that time, which was at the Bel-Air home of Ginger Rogers, the famous song and dance star and partner of Fred Astaire during the forties. Clay was a mysterious surface, which slowed the ball down, allowing the ball to hang in the air, changing the rhythm of play. I liked the clay, yet I never learned to slide on it. Now you have players who are masters at sliding and can even slide on hard courts, doing the splits in the process.

The prior year, a friend of mine from Arizona won this championship, mostly because nobody in our 15-and-under division knew about it. In those days the divisions were divided by age, 11-and-under, 15-and-under, and 18-and-under. Once the rest of us got wind that there was a national championship, all of the top players in that division converged on Chicago.

Chicago's weather in the summer was even worse than that of Bakersfield because it had very heavy humidity. There was no air-conditioning or even a swamp cooler. The conditions for sleeping and playing were difficult.

I made it to the semi-finals and played against a clever girl from Mexico whom none of us had ever heard of. She could hit touch shots and volleys like a pro. The match was long and the summer heat was blistering, sending streams of sweat down our arms and legs. The red clay was everywhere, covering our socks and marking our skirts where we'd wipe our hands. In the third set her father, sitting on the sidelines, began coaching her in Spanish... highly unethical and certainly against the rules. No one could prove it because no one on the Tournament Committee spoke Spanish. She won and went on to win the tournament. Disappointment set in, not just by me, but the whole family. I tried to make excuses, just couldn't come up with any. That year, I was ranked #1 in the 15-and-under division nationally because the Mexican girl could not be ranked in the U.S.

U.S. #1 Fifteen-year-old

25 years later with Rosie Darmon at International 40s Championship

Later she became my good friend. Her name was Rose Maria Reyes. She went on to play tennis internationally, and eventually married another very fine player, Pierre Darmon from France, who became the tournament director of the French Open Championships in Paris, which he ran for years.

Getting Ready

1958 was a good year for me. I was getting ready for bigger and better challenges. More trips to L.A. eventually led to my traveling for the first time to London to play in the Junior Division, along with the Woman's Division, at Wimbledon.

I was flying on an inaugural polar route flight that stopped in Greenland. There were no non-stop flights to London at that time. It took endless hours to reach London in those propeller days. We travelled in full attire... suits, heels, nylons, gloves, and hats. As uncomfortable as it was, it was appropriate. It was expected. It was particularly uncomfortable for someone like me who was used to moving freely and wearing little.

On my way with Janet Hopps and only 3 rackets

London in those days looked like it does today, only with fewer people. London doesn't seem to change, and neither does Wimbledon. Its traditions were rigidly in place then – white-only for tennis clothes. The grass courts were revered and lovingly cared for by the groundskeepers. I had practiced only once on a grass court prior to my London trip. It was on the only grass court that anyone knew of in California. The court was on a golf course in Palm Springs that belonged to the major league baseball player Ralph Kiner and his wife Nancy Chaffee, a former top tennis player in the

1940s. Neither could advise me on how to handle grass court play with balls that don't bounce and those that do, but move in erratic ways.

That year I lost in the first round at Wimbledon in the Women's Division, but won the Juniors easily. I played against a pretty Russian girl, Anna Dmitriva, winning 6-0, 6-2. It was the first time that Russians had competed internationally. They also sent over a boy who played against Butch Buchholotz in the finals of the Boys' Division. These kids travelled with an aggressive propaganda guy who was passing out CCCP (an abbreviation for the USSR) buttons and stickers to whomever would take them. Nikita Khrushchev was running Russia at that time and kept the country isolated from the rest of the world. This tournament was a real step forward in allowing these young players to participate in international competition. There were a couple of chaperones accompanying them, who were hovering over them at all times, concerned that western thinking would contaminate their wards and the kids would try to defect. Years later the great Czech champion Martina Navratilova did just that. Her defection opened the door for Russian players to do the same.

After our wins against the two Russians and in a gesture of friendship, Butch and I were invited to Russia to play exhibition tennis with their stars. We were excited about it, thinking what a great experience this would be until the U.S. U-2 pilot Gary Powers, flying a reconnaissance mission over the Soviet Union airspace, was shot down and held captive. The U.S. State Department said "No" to the invitation we'd received, fearing that once we landed, they weren't sure we would be able to get out. Now Russian tennis players come and go at will, as do the American players in return. It's a sport without boundaries.

After Wimbledon that year, I played and won the U.S. Junior Championships on the grass courts at the Philadelphia Cricket Club. It was really anti-climactic because at that time I was only playing adult women's events. Nevertheless, it felt good to accomplish this goal on the way to the big one. My father was pleased.

National Junior Champion at the Philadelphia Cricket Club

My father continued to be pleased, as I was runner-up to the great, African-American tennis star Althea Gibson in both the Merion and South Orange Championships.

The latter is recorded for posterity in Alfred Hitchcock's North by Northwest film in which Cary Grant, sitting in a taxi in the beginning of the film, holds up a newspaper. There are two pictures of me from the finals of that tournament at

Orange on the back page of the newspaper. For a millisecond I was in the arms of the handsomest man on earth.

Althea and I won the doubles title at South Orange (the prize for each of us was a leather jewelry box), and Maria Bueno and I became runners-up in the U.S. National Doubles Championships at Longwood. The prize there was a little bronze medal, which has since been lost.

With Althea after our long 3-set match at Merion

Black was not the color of tennis clothing or tennis players in the fifties, except for people like those delightful people I knew at Jastro Park. So, when Althea dared to enter the tournaments and play at the most exclusive clubs in the country, there was a bit of a stir – certainly not by the players, rather by members of these elitist clubs. Again, as a rather non-thinking young person, I hardly noticed the stress that this outstanding African-American athlete was under and the barriers she was breaking. I saw her only as my competitor, someone whom I wanted to beat. Not too easy a task. She was tall and strong and she could serve and volley, a rare ability then.

*

To win means something,

but to do the best you can is the ultimate.

*

I always tried my best. It was the way I was trained... never to quit or give up. It didn't occur to me to do otherwise. I may not have won every match I played, but I gave my all every time I stepped on the court.

8 MORE LEARNING

And School?

As I look back, I feel it was a lovely way to spend my youth – focusing on tennis – better than what most kids my age in Bakersfield concentrated on. In truth, it never occurred to me at the time whether it was lovely or not. It was just what I did.

Naturally, all kids went to school. It's what you did after school that separated us. High school had its highlights – art classes. Bakersfield High had the best art teachers. Crazy Mrs. Emerson, who split a button and glued the pieces to the edges of her glasses for adornment, extended my oil painting skills in her oil painting class. Can you imagine being taught oil painting in a public high school? How clever and creative she was! We all loved her for her oddities, and her enthusiasm in sharing what she knew – art.

Mr. Krumb was also an inventive fellow who had us making books and fancy portfolios out of heavy cardboard and paper mache. He spoke to us of serious matters too. He said that we, his students, would have the privilege of experiencing the turn of a century. He would not. He must have been in his mid-forties then. I remembered him on the day the twentieth century rolled into the twenty-first. I wondered if any of his other students did too.

I stumbled through French but excelled in biology only because my teacher needed a large demonstration piece to explain the life cycle of the Chinese liver fluke. She knew I could paint. So, she gave me a huge map-sized canvas to work on, and passed me with high marks when I turned in a stunning illustration of this unattractive subject. Then again, she had something she could use for years. It was a good trade.

High school was nothing I relished. It was a huge school with 5,000 students and not all of them interested in education. There were gang wars on campus with white gangs and black gangs dueling and threatening each other every other week or so. When the word would go out that a rumble was in the making, I maintained a low profile and stayed out of the way. I had my goal and my only pleasure through those four years were the few art classes on my schedule.

Following my Brother

Bob paved the way for my higher education. He was a student at Occidental College and in a fraternity. He enticed me there while I was still in high school by setting me up for a date with a fraternity brother of his to go to a fancy prom. Sorority girls dressed me in a fluffy evening gown, heels, and make up. The evening was divine and my heart was set on Oxy.

My tennis accomplishments and a great reference from

our local minister who had graduated from Occidental cemented my entrance. Certainly, it was not my grades. There were, of course, no scholarships for women athletes at any school, let alone at a small school like Oxy. My father footed the bill.

Occidental was a sweet school, the first choice for those who did not get into Stanford. The campus was lovely with eucalyptus trees whose fragrance drifted in the air enhancing the setting. Again, it was the art classes that held my interest – painting, design, art history, and drawing classes.

I loved the art classes and the professors. I felt at home in the art department, which was housed in a building separate from the rest of the campus. The art students were the bohemians of the school, the elitists in their own way. They would have been hippies, but it was before flower children came into vogue.

"Change," I would yell when I was put in charge of a model's poses in a life drawing class. "Change again," I would call out after 10, 20 or 30 seconds. It took only that long to put the essence of a pose down on a piece of paper, and that was the most important part of any painting or drawing – that initial impression. Paint fast, draw fast, don't think. Do it!

Besides art, my school days were filled with usual social activities of fraternity events, sorority parties – and spontaneous skateboard/beer gatherings on the local hilly sidewalks of Pasadena. You could not buy a skateboard in a store. They didn't exist. This was the beginning of that industry and its sister, snowboarding. The original skateboard was created by surfers, of which my Oxy boyfriend was one. These early skateboarders would take a short 2x4 piece of wood, spread and attach one skate to it with hammer and nails. The skate was from one of those old skates that used a key to tighten it to your shoe. Such a skate was dangerous on your shoe and even more dangerous when it was hammered onto a 2x4. Down the hill we would sail, filled with enough beer to make the inevitable crash tolerable. I was a typical college girl at that time, except that I had a particular goal that I was working for. My interest in skateboarding and the surfer/skateboarder faded as I continued my quest.

Tennis was never out of sight while I was at Oxy. Many days after classes, I would drive to the Los Angeles Tennis Club and work out with George. The goal was still intact, but work was necessary to achieve it.

Winner of Ojai Tournament with runner-up Janet Hopps

As the school year came to a close, the spring tournament season ramped up. Regional tournaments prepared me for the big one in late June. I was sailing along, winning the Ojai Championship and the Southern California Championship before flying to England. I won two tournaments in Northern England, prior to the final warm up tournament at Queens Club, and this entitled me to a good spot in the Wimbledon draw. That's when my game fell apart with the uneven bounces on the rough and raggedy grass courts at Queens, which left me with an equally rough and raggedy forehand.

I called George, but there was hardly anything he could do over the phone. I struggled on, winning in any way I could… until I reached the semi-finals. And that's how I eventually ended up on Center Court at Wimbledon playing against Maria Bueno in the semifinals… and losing.

Starting Again

There was only one solution to this disastrous situation: George! I hustled back to L.A. to spend another intensive week re-grooving my/George's forehand.

Starting from the beginning once again, George patiently dropped balls to my forehand side, refreshing my memory on how the stroke should be formed, just as he did when I was a beginner. Many balls later, the process moved to ball machines, lobbing balls to me, very slowly at first. I don't know why I kept on this tennis path, but I had nothing else. I was a tennis player. I was still on my way to becoming champion, I believed. This is what it took, so I did it. I had to do it. There was no way around it. There was also no pleasure in it, except the encouraging words from George. I certainly needed them.

In Chicago with Perry T. Jones, Mary Hardwick Hare and the Davis Cup, evidently too bright to keep my eyes open

Finally, I could rally again, hitting harder and harder. At last, it was back; my forehand was solid. A week later I flew to Chicago and won the National Clay Court Championships. The effort was worth it. It always was. That's what it took – effort. It took effort to get anywhere or accomplish anything. I put in the effort.

The effort continued to yield results, but nerves were always a factor for me. In those days no one bothered about such things. No one travelled with a coach, a trainer, and certainly not a sports psychologist.

We were tennis players, not athletes. Training, if you were really serious, consisted of a bit of running or jumping rope. No one thought of lifting weights or reprogramming your psychological structure for winning. You just went out and played.

Years later when my husband and I had become members of the PGA West Tennis Club in La Quinta, California, there was a group of old duffers with whom I played a weekly doubles match on the clay courts. I would prance onto the court and never fail to remind them that I was once National Clay Court Champion. This started the joking and teasing. I think that's why I have always preferred playing men's doubles to ladies' doubles to this day. Men looked at a match as the opportunity for a verbal jesting duel, whereas women just played tennis.

*

Honor your past. Honor your future.

Honor yourself. Take a bow!

*

Perhaps I could stop for a moment to enjoy what I had accomplished. Then again, perhaps not. There was more to do.

9 A SWEETER GOAL

A Change of Heart

1960 caught me in a bad state health-wise during the school year at Occidental. I had awakened early one morning with intense stomach pain. No over-the-counter remedy would alleviate it. George was my surrogate father in the L.A. area and was the one I called for help. He dealt with numerous doctors who were members of the LATC and he gave me the name of one. I didn't wait for the doctor's office to open. I just lay outside his door until someone arrived.

"You have a massive ovarian cyst," announced the doctor. Do you want to be operated on here or in Bakersfield?"

The next day, I had abdominal surgery in Bakersfield. It took twenty-one days for tissue to heal, I was told, so there was still the possibility of making the tennis season in Europe. In my eagerness to make that trip, I proceeded to overdo it during the recovery period and contracted mononucleosis. Everyone in school seemed to get mono in those days.

Nevertheless, by the time the next tennis season rolled around I was finally in top form and was perfectly poised to reach my life-long dream of becoming "the champion." I was strong, healthy, and fully recovered from the surgery. I had a forehand, and was ready for action. Or, so I thought.

I arrived in England prepared to continue where I'd left off the year before. Once again, I travelled alone. The first warm-up tournament to Wimbledon was Manchester. As the prior year's winner, I was seeded number one in the draw. The seeding didn't faze the girl I played in the first round. She beat me handily. I was out of the tournament on the first day. This was not supposed to happen. This was not in my playbook. I tried to rack it up to the fact that I wasn't "tournament tough." I didn't really buy this excuse, but it was all that I could come up with.

The weather was as miserable as my mood. I sulked around the tournament grounds until a couple of Argentina players asked me to join them for dinner. Typical of many of the Latin guys, the dialog slid into raunchy. I left.

I returned to my room in the Midland Hotel and got into bed. It was a small bed in a tall room with dreary drapes, again fitting my mood. A call to my parents was necessary. My mother wished me a happy birthday. It was my twentieth. Their disappointment matched mine. This was to be my year. What went wrong? No matter, there was still the goal ahead. There was still Wimbledon. All was not lost.

That's the way it was in those days, everything hinged on winning or losing. One's whole life revolved around success or lack of it, at least for me it did. What a waste, I later came to understand. What a limited point of view of life it was. But that's the way it was then. If you were a player, winning was everything. Your self-worth was all wrapped up in it.

With nothing better to do, I sat in bed and I started thinking about the last 24 hours, a day of loss and disappointment. If I had to color it, it would have been gray, dark gray. As I thought about it, I decided that this was no way to spend my birthday.

I checked the clock. I still had fifteen minutes before the dining room closed. I jumped out of bed, threw on my favorite cover-up over my pajamas, rolled up my pajama legs, tossed a string of pearls around my neck, put on my patent leather pumps, a pair of gloves and headed out the door. The cover-up was a long, black sweater coat with twenty buttons in two rows down the front. It took me the entire elevator ride down to the main floor to get them all fastened. When I stepped out of the elevator, I was perfectly presentable.

The maître d' was none too enthusiastic to see me coming. He was ready to close shop. The dining room was elegant and empty at this late hour, except for one romantic couple sipping an after-dinner drink by candlelight.

I took my time; this was my birthday dinner and I planned to enjoy it. Plaice to start the meal, then lamb chops, vegetables, and a salad would be just fine. The waiter was antsy; he wanted to end his shift too. He didn't realize what a special day this was, and I wasn't willing to let his discomfort spoil my enjoyment.

When I left the dining room and ambled down the

hallway of the hotel, I heard familiar music coming from a side salon. It was from the musical *Bye Bye Birdie*, a fun spoof on Elvis Presley and the occasion of his being drafted into the Army. I knew it by heart. I had been given a copy of the album when I was in the hospital and later used it to jump rope to while training for this trip.

Jumping rope to the records of musicals had been the only way to make the mundane chore of my limited training somewhat bearable. It was almost like dancing and I really liked to dance. I had jumped along, creating special routines for *Oklahoma, Annie Get Your Gun, My Fair Lady, The Sound of Music, Gigi,* and more. There was hardly a musical of which I didn't know the lyrics.

So here I was listening to the music I loved. Naturally, I wandered into the corridor toward the sound and found a seat. I was behind some curtains so that no one could see me. The words in the song were different, altered for the occasion, I presumed, but the music was the same. It had a warming feeling, hearing this happy music on such a dismal day.

When a waitress finally discovered me, I asked her what was going on. "It's the cast of *Bye Bye Birdie*. They are in town preparing for their London opening," she said. "It's one of the writer's birthday."

Well, I couldn't contain myself, "It's my birthday too!" I blurted out.

With that she left and returned with the star of the show. Now, Peter at that time was about as good looking as any man I'd ever seen – thirty-five, tall, dark, big smile, flashing eyes, warm voice, and a razzle dazzle that struck me dumb. It was his excited way of speaking… a bit nervous, a bit eager… that got me. He was enthusiastic and magnetic. I was caught up in his irresistible charm.

Of course, I was escorted into the party where sparkling lights and colorful paper hats dressed up the festivities. I enjoyed a piece of birthday cake and was introduced to the other birthday celebrant, Charles Strouse, along with Chita Rivera, who was playing the other lead in the musical, and her then husband choreographer Tony Mordente. And then there was Peter Marshall – I was sunk! I had the added pleasure of knowing that I was sitting there in my pajamas and no one was any the wiser.

From that moment on, tennis took a back seat to love, or more precisely… romance.

During my high school and college years, my heart was stolen away now and then by darling young men who could play tennis well or dance with grace. Even a short flirtation with Ricky Nelson tickled my heart for a moment or two. Ricky was part of the then famous Ozzie Nelson family that had its own television show for years, until he broke out on its own and became a rock star. I knew him when he was more or less young and innocent… but he could dance, really dance. He taught me "The Chicken," the fastest footwork anybody could do on a dance floor.

For some reason, I had always been attracted to "stars," no matter their arena they were in. Perhaps it was my exposure to the L.A. Tennis Club's membership when I was an impressionable teenager that tweaked this admiration, this "awe." That club was filled with them: Charlton Heston of Ben

Hur fame, Vera Ellen who co-starred with Bing Crosby in the classic *White Christmas* film, Raymond Burr, the star of TV's long-running Perry Mason and Ironside series, and many more. Only later, did I realize that "stars" shine brightly mostly because of the light that others shine on them.

But this was my first real grown-up romance. And, it was right out of a musical.

It is interesting how these things happen. I had been listening to and loving musicals for years, and was especially captivated by the romance inherent in each play. They seemed to speak to my starry-eyed heart. In all my daydreaming while jumping rope, was it possible that had I created or attracted this musical romance?

With Jack Jones who had a big heart

Many years later I thought about this theme in regard to a friend of mine, Jack Jones, a wonderful jazz, pop singer, who had his heyday in the sixties.

Throughout his life, during his many concerts, Jack sang love songs… falling in love, breaking up, getting back together, unrequited love… just love, love, love. And how did his life go? He married six times. I believe that can happen – when you think about something and feel it deeply, life can make it happen.

But with Peter at this point, I wasn't thinking about how I got there. I liked where I was. I had arrived in my mind. Romance was everything at this point. What could be better than love? Obviously, I'd gotten attraction, romance, and love all mixed up. However, at that moment, a happier girl, you could not find.

Peter and I spent evenings together after his rehearsals and my workouts. I was still getting ready for the big one – Wimbledon, just in a more lackadaisical manner. How that was going to work out I couldn't say. I didn't seem to care. What I cared about was the man, not boy, in my life with his arm around my shoulders or his hand touching my cheek as we talked of nothing that seemed to matter.

There was just one hitch to this romantic picture – my parents. In their desire to watch me win Wimbledon this year, and it was pretty much assured that I would, they had borrowed money to fly to London. On top of that, we were scheduled to stay together at a friends' home in London. The friends were lovely people, a doctor and his wife, who had a four-story flat that housed his medical practice along with their living quarters.

As I prepared for the Championships, my heart wasn't into tennis. It was with Peter. My competitive spirit had melted. Using the craftiness, probably learned on the tennis court, I somehow convinced my parents that I was not comfortable staying in this home and needed more privacy. This, of course, was a crock. I should have been honest and more respectful, if I'd thought about it. But I wasn't thinking and definitely not about all they had done for me. I should have, but I wasn't. I was selfishly feeling quite wonderful. Who isn't when you're in love?

Wanting me to be in the best mental/emotional state for the tournament, my parents allowed me to find lodging elsewhere. That I did. What I found was a cozy little one-room flat a short distance from the Majestic Theater where Peter was performing. This meant that I spent evenings lying to my parents that I needed to go to bed early, and scooting out from underneath their scrutiny to rendezvous with my song and dance man. Once I was on my own, Peter and I dined at intimate cafés, walked the streets of Soho hand in hand where he would occasionally stop, turn to me and burst into song. It was right out of *My Fair Lady*!

*

Life sings only love songs.

*

I believe that's all I heard at this point in my life.

10 BREAKING A PROMISE

Dropping the Ball

Of course, all this romancing and late nights left my tennis in shambles. As a last year's semi-finalist, my first round match this year was scheduled for Court One, a prime court for tennis fans.

On Court One with an unimpressive performance

As I entered the stadium, my nervous system was more erratic than ever. I was not fully prepared mentally or physically for this match. I hadn't truly been working out seriously and my mind was in the clouds, along with my heart.

My parents sat with Peter in the stands, not understanding what he meant to me other than just a friend I had met in Manchester.

During the warm up, I broke a fingernail. Was this an omen? The ballboy fetched a piece of tape for me. I remember being more concerned about having broken that nail and how my hair looked than winning the match. After all, these were the essentials in what I considered important now. As the play began, I knew that a first round loss would not sit well with my parents, my father especially – and it did not. My performance was less than stellar. My opponent was not impressive; I was less so. My heart definitely wasn't in it, yet I was not particularly heart-broken about it. But they were.

This situation required foregoing my usual pattern of deception. I needed to dine with my parents that evening. There was no way to avoid it. Sitting together in the restaurant, the mood was somber, the tension was thick and strained. All that my father and I had worked on for years had come to nothing and there was no valid explanation I could give to alleviate their disappointment. It wasn't just the disappointment in my having lost the match; it was a disappointment in me. They had given me so much and I had not responded in kind. It had been a huge effort, years of effort. I was saddened for them, not for myself. My father's face was especially revealing… tired, unhappy, displeased. For the first time, I'd found myself on the wrong side of him. That was hard to take. It was not in the words that were exchanged, it was in the feelings that passed between us. I can't remember the exact words my father said, but they were filled with disappointment. At that moment, it was as if someone had died in their eyes. Me! Perhaps that day tennis died for all of us.

My parents left immediately for home. I had a few doubles matches yet to play, so I stayed on. Still oblivious to the depths of my deceit or not wanting to dwell on it, I continued to be a young woman in love who was now free to attend the fabulous Wimbledon Ball at the end of the tournament... with Peter.

A postcard was made of each player

After the curtain went down on his evening performance of *Birdie,* Peter entered the ballroom at the Mayfair Hotel in a stunningly handsome tuxedo, looking like the star he was. I was beyond proud to be with him and madly in love with him. What a silly girl! Of course, goals change, but was this a worthy one? Was this one that would yield good results? With my amorous heart unleashed, what else was there to think about? Such focus on this sport throughout my life had left me vulnerable to the ways of the world. I was certainly unprepared for the ways of love.

I shed more than a few salty tears during our last tender moments together before we said our goodbyes. His show was a hit and he had to remain in London, and I had to leave for a previously scheduled trip through Italy. This separation was always in the background of our relationship as being inevitable, but until I faced it in real time, I didn't know how much it would hurt. And it did. The loss of love is never a joyous experience. The truth was obvious – that there was no future with this leading man, no matter that he was so amusing and enchanting, so delicious and charming; he already had a family back in California. I had to move on. Wimbledon was over in many ways.

A Wimbledon Aside

In the days that I participated at Wimbledon, there was not just the hardcore, serious tennis played as it is today. There were also some lighter moments. One of these occurred before the beginning of the tournament each year. It was a social event not only for the players but also for the upper crust of London society, with a few royals thrown in. It was held at the exclusive, private sports and social facility called The Hurlingham Club, which consisted of a large Georgian clubhouse and 42 acres of gorgeous gardens and grounds set in the center of London. To this day, there is a thirty-year waiting list for membership. Golf, cricket, bowls, skittles, squash, croquet, and lawn tennis were all played there through the centuries.

On the Sunday prior to the start of the Wimbledon fortnight, all the tournament players gathered to play social doubles and have tea with the membership and their friends... and see what that particular year's new attire would be. It was a fashion show!

This was right up Teddy Tinling's alley. He took the opportunity each year to present his new line of tennis dresses with his gang of eight top women players flaunting his creations.

Exhibition tennis on the "lawns" of Hurlingham

On one of the most memorable years, he dressed all of his "models," including me, in paper and glass! That is, the dresses were made of a rather heavy paper, yet just as finely tailored as if they were of linen. Each girl's dress was trimmed in ribbon in a different color. Mine was yellow. Now the glass part of the ensemble was fiberglass. It was an unusually light and flowing fiberglass fabric designed as a duster to go over the dress. And true to Teddy's artistic nature, it was trimmed in the same ribbon and trim color as the dress.

Teddy had the idea that the women who shopped at Harrods or Lillywhites, who usually bought his frocks, would prefer to throw a dress away rather than wash it. This was his big surprise at Hurlingham that year.

Also present was Fred Perry and his wreaths, that are famously part of his logo. He was always trying to compete with Teddy. So, this particular year, he kept under wraps what his new line would be. Not until the day of the big Hurlingham party was it revealed – MINK! He trimmed the sexiest Italian player, Lea Pericoli in a simple tennis dress trimmed on the bottom of the skirt and around the neck with mink. It was ugly and almost as silly as paper and glass!

There was one more light-hearted outing for players during the fortnight. It occurred on the middle Sunday. All the players, men and women, piled into buses and were driven out of town to a fabulous park where a picnic of food and drink awaited us. But it wasn't the refreshments that attracted the male players. It was the soccer! Top tennis players from around the world took sides and proceeded to have at it. The Australians – Roy Emerson, Rod Laver, Mal Anderson, Lew Hoad, and John Newcombe – ganged up on the Spaniards, Mexicans, French, and Italians – Manuel Santana, Niki Pietrangeli, Pierre Darmon, Antonio Palafox. Even the Swedes jumped in – Sven Davidson, Ulf Schmidt, and Torben Ulrich. Where were the Americans? Standing on the sidelines watching. Soccer was not yet popular in the U.S. Kids were not rounded up and enrolled in soccer camps at that time. Can you imagine a Federer or Djokovic risking a twisted ankle?

We also had fun moments on the courts. In those days

every player played in the singles, doubles and mixed doubles events. After the serious singles play, there was always the light-hearted competition of doubles and mixed doubles. I had the honor of playing against one of the greats from the past – Henri Cochet. Henri was then 61 years old. But he had been the world number one ranked player in the late 1920s and was one of the "Four Musketeers." This group of rapscallions consisted of the renowned members of the French Davis Cup Team at that time: Rene Lacoste, Toto Brugnon, and Jean Borotra. They were famous for their antics of soaking the red clay courts in Paris before the Americans arrived for a Davis Cup match, thus slowing the courts beyond reason and assuring a French win.

Henri Cochet still a Wimbledon competitor at 61

However, each year the Wimbledon committee honored Cochet for his past achievements by allowing him to play in the mixed doubles event. He always drew a crowd and it was fun to play against him.

I had enjoyed Wimbledon and my romance but now I

needed a change.

Italian Escape

When sadness sets in change the landscape. Change the mood. Just change something and I did. Fortunately, I had already arranged a trip to Italy, again one that my father financed.

Through a friend at Occidental College, I had become acquainted with a bon vivant in Rome. All three hundred pounds of George Seabury were energetic and outrageously entertaining. He was the top PR guy with the biggest airline at the time, Pan Am. And he hosted everyone who was anyone who visited Rome. This included me.

Over-looking the Rome cityscape from George's terrace

I met George in Rome where he organized a whirlwind tour of Venice with stops in between. "Go to Harry's Bar," he said, "and introduce yourself to Arrigo Cippriani." Arrigo was owner of the bar as well as the grand, luxurious Cipriani Hotel, where I would be staying. "And, be sure to have a peach Bellini at Harry's," George insisted.

Wanting to please George, on my first day in Venice I put on a sassy, summer frock, and flirty Italian sandals and headed for Harry's. Playing my new role as a femme fatale, although not a very experienced one, I walked along the strata toward the bar. I felt marvelous! I felt like a star in my own movie, perhaps emulating Ingrid Bergman or Sophia Loren. I was now a young woman who could function in any arena, I thought. Powerful, yes that's how I felt – powerful and carefree as I strutted along the strata. The air was a musty mix of the dampness from the canals, coffee from the little cafes, and the earthy fragrance of germaniums that decorated doorways along the way.

The entrance to Harry's Bar is at the end of the narrow Calle Vallaressso, just a few feet from the Grand Canal. Arrigo, son of the original owner, was watching through a window, he later told me. Before I could open the door, he was standing in the doorway to greet me... graciously with calculated charm. The room was small, elegant with cramped tables and in a suave, subdued beige-on-white décor. Altogether Italian. I sat with this charming man, so Italian, romantic and sexy – and took in the atmosphere. After a few exchanges, plus the greetings that I passed along from George, Arrigo ordered two Bellinis. It was fluffy, light and delicious. Its pretty rose color was topped with a creamy, frothy head. I sipped it. It was spectacular as was the company.

Back at the hotel, a large contingent of college girls had arrived. They were making their "grand tour" of Europe. When I came downstairs to the hotel lobby the next morning, they were all atwitter as preparing for a day of sailing. Like the Marlborough girls, these girls had all the earmarks of the affluent – no worries and no concern for anything except enjoyment. At the same time they were hopping onto their sailboat, I was being helped aboard a Chriscraft speedboat with Arrigo at the helm. Off we flew past the sailboat and the girls. Was I still competing? I thought that without a moment's hesitation, any of them would have switched places with me.

We spent the day exploring the ruins on his family's island, Torcello, as Arrigo filled me in on its history and ushered me around the sights. Twelve parishes, sixteen cloisters and numerous palazzi entertained the tourists of which I was now one. Torcello was where Arrigo's father used to hunt with Ernest Hemingway and where Hemingway wrote his novel *Across the River and Through the Trees.* The air was soft, slightly moist with a few floating clouds. We lunched on pears, prosciutto, and wine under an arbor at his family's restaurant, Locanda Cipriani near the Byzantine Cathedral of Santa Maria Dell'Assunta. Sweet words were spoken there, but nothing that had to do with a future. It was a delightful dalliance, that's all. After lunch as we motored back to the hotel, we waved to the girls in the sailboat as we passed. They looked tired and hot from their day in the sun. It was a lovely day, but sadly Arrigo was another man with a family.

Next on the itinerary that George had created for me was Florence. I took in everything that any art student would. Still, I was more enchanted by the yellow roses that Arrigo sent.

I wandered around the historic sites of that great city, paying more attention to the miraculous colors of the city's weathered walls than the Renaissance masterpieces. Certainly, there was Michelangelo's David sculpture and Botticelli's "The birth of Venus" and da Vinci's "Annunciation." But it was the walls, to me, that gave the city, and most of the Italian cities I visited, their allure, their flavor. The terracotta colors were the result of centuries of sun and rain on a Mediterranean Coast.

Returning to Rome, George had still another outing scheduled – this time to his friend's villa on the Mediterranean. The place was loaded with characters all of whom ended up playing themselves the next year in Fellini's stylish cinematic landmark *La Doce Vita* (the sweet life,) a film about social decadence. As amusing as they were, indulging themselves and flaunting their excesses, these folks were something to be observed from a distance. However, it was the magnificent vistas of the deep cyan blue Mediterranean that captured my attention.

For George's next excursion it included both of us -- visiting the home of Pompeo Maresi on Lake Como. The Maresi's had a fabulous villa with a boathouse. Their guesthouse, referred to as the Maresi Hilton, was bigger than most villas. The grounds included a pool and a clay tennis court, both of which were surrounded by pine trees and overlooked the lake. The Maresi's invited me to join them on the Queen Mary as a sort of an overseer of their precocious twin daughters. The family was wending their way back to their home in Tuxedo Park, New York, where they were to deliver one of their Rolls-Royces to their son as a wedding gift. First-class was the only way the Maresi's travelled. The family occupied the royal suite. Our luggage room was larger than most every cabin.

The twelve-year-old girls were high-spirited and adventurous and ran circles around their parents. It didn't matter whether they were in Como, the family ski lodge in St. Moritz, or on the Queen Mary, they were a handful.

But the high-life was strange and unsettling to me. I was not used to parents who fought and drank, nor was I accustomed to children who tried to escape their parents at every turn. Somehow, I'd forgotten about my own deceptive antics earlier in the summer. So, I returned to the balanced sanity of my own family in search of a new direction.

*

We sail through life as life sails through us.

*

I seem to have lost my rudder. I needed to find it. Home was the answer.

11 NO GOAL

Entering Hollywood

My father and I had a final pow-wow with Coach George to try to figure out what I should do next. I was confused and a bit apprehensive about this change. My identity was as a tennis player, what would happen if I just quit? Who would I be then? Where was my heart? Certainly not in tennis. It is so hard to do anything when your heart is not in it. The truth is there had been no preparation for anything other than tennis in my life. This is a warning for those who are planning on a champion's path: have a backup plan. I had none and I think I was weaker or at least more vulnerable for having been so one-dimensionally focused.

Delicately, my two fathers maneuvered me around to agreeing that I should put my competitive rackets away for six months and if I wanted to return to tennis, I could. That was it. I was free. That's how I felt. I'm not sure how my father felt. My tennis had been such a huge part of his life. It had been time taken away from my mother and my brother. I was grateful, though probably not enough, but I needed to find my own way. I appreciated that. They were giving me the room to do it.

A wise and thoughtful father with his daughter

I certainly could not return to Bakersfield, having had a taste of the "good life." I set up my base camp in a less-than-glamorous, one-room apartment near the Peppermint West Lounge in Hollywood. My activities were none too worthy or noteworthy: I played social tennis during the day and danced all night. I had no direction or goal... no Wimbledon. I had been so goal-oriented through my life so far, now I just took a break and went with the flow. I did what I felt like with no particular purpose. And, I did it with great abandon. My means of support, as I remember, was still my father.

On one of those dancing nights, "twisting again like we did last summer," my eye caught a party entering the Peppermint Lounge. It was the well-known entertainer Jimmy Durante, Peter with a woman, whom I assumed was his wife, and Peter's sister, the 40s and 50s film actress Joanne Dru, plus a few others. I was dumbstruck, not expecting to ever see this man again. When our paths crossed in the noise and chaos of the nightclub, he took my phone number and our "friendship" renewed. There followed trips to watch him perform in shows here and there up and down California and Las Vegas. Still, there was nothing promised, nothing expected.

Standing on my own Feet

Bakersfield remained my home base for balance. It was simple, steady, and supportive. I would drive up to Bakersfield on a whim to visit my parents and be nourished in all ways. I would tell them about my life, skirting the racy parts, and play a bit of golf with my father. When he could see that I could connect with the ball easily, he wanted me to take some golf lessons. No, I'd done that. No more lessons of any kind. My mother would toss a tasty green salad and my father would barbecue a steak for dinner. He ate barbecued meat nearly every night for years. Little did we know then that would literally be the death of him.

About this time, a friend introduced me to Ralph Story, also a tennis player and a very popular Los Angeles TV personality who had his own show – Ralph Story's Los Angeles. He was a sweetheart of a guy with a whimsical sense of humor... kind of like the TV personality Mister Rogers, wholesome only with humor. Ralph's assistant was forced to leave her position for some medical reason and I was invited by Ralph to step in. Why not?

Ralph was writing a book about L.A. and he asked me to gather the research for this project. The hours were loose, which suited me, as did the opportunity to visit all sorts of interesting venues in the area. They consisted of everything from exclusive restaurants to dinghy hot dog stands to private dance clubs, and to tattoo parlors, fancy day spas and sleazy bathhouses. I roamed from Olivera Street and Chinatown in downtown Los Angeles to Beverly Hills, the Hollywood hills, and Malibu.

My opening line was: "I'm Ralph Story's assistant. Ralph is doing a book on Los Angeles and would like to include your business/establishment/operation/nightclub in it. May I speak with the owner/manager/chef/dance instructor?" Within minutes a senior representative would show up and treat me to a lovely meal/workout/evening of dance/bar's specialty. I then prepared a few notes on the subject for Ralph and I was done.

Playing with handsome, successful Seth Baker in Palm Springs

I continued to use this line long after I left Ralph's employment and would still receive royal treatment any where I went.

Where did this boldness and brashness come from? It was a confidence that certainly didn't come from my days in Bakersfield, or did it? Having achieved a degree of success on the tennis court at a young age might have cultivated it. It didn't hurt that I was young and somewhat attractive. Self-confidence was definitely not lacking. I was game for most anything.

*

The days we keep are the days we are thankful for.

*

At this point, I had a lot to be thankful for, probably more than I realized.

12 HOLLYWOOD LIFE

A Love Match

Over the years, I have learned that tennis is the greatest entrée you could have. My ability to play opened many doors for me throughout my life. One of the best was a gate to a tennis court in Beverly Hills.

The court was connected to a mansion, up from the Beverly Hills Hotel, on the side of a hill that was nestled above a ravine filled with eucalyptus trees. The court was owned by a well-known motion picture mogul, Samuel Goldwyn. It was totally private, except for the peering eyes of Mr. Goldwyn far above.

This court came to be one of my favorites places to play. The scent of eucalyptus floating up from the trees below created a heavenly atmosphere. Cement walls encompassed three sides of the court, which made the sound of the ball reverberate, mimicking a center court stadium. I loved this. It was grand. It was luxurious. Everything smacked of quality.

My then boyfriend had brought me there to play social tennis with a group of Hollywood elites. The boyfriend was a fine young man who had given me an engagement ring, although I wasn't all that committed to this union. When my mother asked, "Should I call the newspaper and make an announcement?" I said, "No, let's wait."

All day long a number of players and I played, rotated in and out of sets. At one point, I had the opportunity to chat with the mogul's son, Sam, Jr., who was a mini mogul in his own right. We sat in the gazebo on the side of the court and talked about a movie he was producing and directing. He was an extremely attractive man, I thought, with an aquiline nose, sandy hair and wore smart tortoise shell aviator glasses. Obviously, he'd come from the freckled, reddish-complexioned line of his Jewish heritage. He also had the look of someone who has been well fed his whole life, healthy with the hint of plumpness. He later told me that during the Great Depression of the 1930s when he was a school-child at Black Fox Military Academy in Los Angele, his mother would send a limousine to the school daily to bring him a hot lunch.

The movie was in pre-production and Sam explained that he needed an amphitheater for one of the locations in his movie. "I know of a beautiful amphitheater," I said. "It's at Occidental College."

Out the door flew the engagement with the boyfriend, and off I went in Sam's sporty Jaguar convertible to explore the site… and more.

Was I an opportunist climbing some elusive ladder? Certainly, in tennis a player learns how to take advantage of situations that are presented, and they are usually presented unexpectedly, like this one. I had no great designs. The truth was that I dared to follow my heart... and not just any heart, my romantic heart. And this man plucked the strings of mine.

What was the attraction? I'm not sure. He was not the most handsome man I had ever met, but he had a grace and stature that appealed to me... and he was smart and quick to laugh uncontrollably. He was easy for me to understand and know, although we had only exchanged a few words. More it seems is known from what is not said than from what is said. I liked what was not said. And so, I stayed in the game.

Movie Magic

The art director on Sam's movie, *The Young Lovers,* which would be starring Peter Fonda, was Richard Day who was then elderly and had fallen and broken his arm. Since Richard could not drive and I knew the Los Angeles area thoroughly, Sam hired me to drive him to do location hunting.

What an opportunity this was for me – to be in the presence of such an outstanding art director and lovely human being! His accomplishments were many. Through the years Richard Day had won seven Academy Awards for his work on films like *A Streetcar Named Desire, On the Waterfront, How Green Was My Valley,* and others. He'd tell me little tidbits from his experiences on films – how Eva Marie Saint had accidentally dropped her glove while walking with Marlon Brando in a scene from *On the Waterfront* and how Marlon had picked it up and fiddled with it so tenderly, making that scene so very memorable. Sharing these moments brought him back to the days when he worked on big films, although this movie was a little one.

As part of my job, I took Richard to students' apartments and art classrooms at the University of Southern California, where I was attending classes in my free time to finish my bachelor's degree. We borrowed easels from one of the classrooms and used instructor Keith Crown's paintings in the film (Crown became quite upset later when we returned his paintings and he found that Peter had actually painted on one.) We even hired my favorite model, Nina, for a scene in which Peter was drawing her nude. I was appalled at how childish the crew members were in viewing the model... sneaking around and "teeheeing." Nudity was nothing new to me. Most of my art classes had nude models. There was no sexuality involved. It made me sad to have exposed Nina to these leering buffoons.

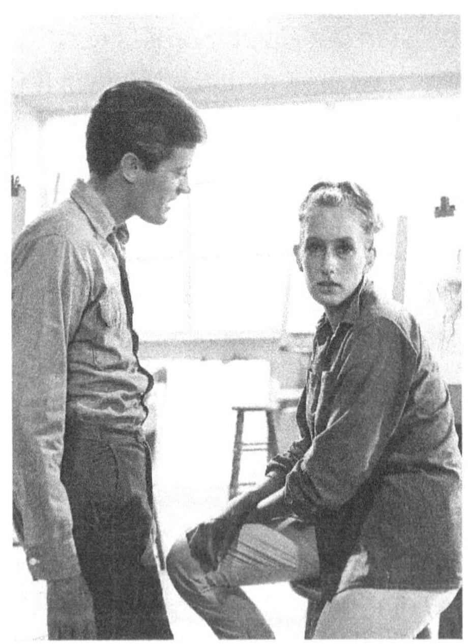

With Peter Fonda on the set of *The Young Lovers*

For days I drove Richard around scouting

neighborhoods, trying to find just the right storefronts and homes for various scenes. I learned about storyboards, set design, and set building. It was all so fascinating – no wonder people wanted to work in the film business.

Then, in the middle of shooting the film, Sam's assistant quit. Again, I filled in. I had no particular skills to be a secretary. I could type and could fumble through dictation, make coffee, and answer the phone. That was it. But it was sufficient.

When Richard's work was done and shooting was under way, I moved back and forth from the office to the sound stage to outside locations, learning about scripts and script supervision, direction, lighting, sound, and wardrobe. I loved working at the studio. Not only could I walk in and out of the stage where Sam's movie was being shot, but I could also walk onto other stages at will.

On the set of *The Young Lovers* with the soundman

One day I watched Elvis romance Ann Margaret on one stage and then walked onto another to see Peter Sellers perform his antics. On still another, there was Marlon Brando getting sprayed in his face while shooting a scene for *Mutiny on the Bounty*. There was always something of interest going on.

Yes, it was fascinating and I learned a great deal. Everyone on a set was willing to share their knowledge; all I had to do was ask. I also learned how to be discreet as the girlfriend of another man who already had a family. What was this pattern and what was I preparing for? Was there any thinking going on? Was there a goal? None of this crossed my mind as I enjoyed every day at the studio.

My heart was now sunk into my romance with Sam. A thirty-five-year-old man and twenty-two-year-old woman seemed to be the perfect age spread to me, whether it was on or off the tennis court. Sam's erudite appearance accompanied an exquisite taste in all things from cars to clothes to movies to music and books, to food and vacations. He just smelled good. There were weekends in La Jolla, Palm Springs, and Sausalito, evenings in Malibu and Brentwood, and a week in New York now and then. I was included in dinner parties with all the "swells."

One in particular stands out. It was at the home of David O. Selznick, the producer of *Gone with the Wind*. His home was on Tower Road, the very road that Elizabeth Taylor's good friend and actor Montgomery Cliff had crashed in a car a couple of years before, nearly ending his career and his life. Everybody knew the story and was wary of the winding road.

Wanting me to attend this gathering, Sam included

best-selling novelist Robert Gover in our party to make my presence more acceptable, I suppose. The party proceeded with attendees such as actress Jane Fonda, and English actor Norman Lloyd, who told wicked stories about his friend Alfred Hitchcock. There seemed to be great excitement when the actress Lauren Bacall showed up. Rex Harrison, who had not yet filmed *My Fair Lady*, was there with his wife the English actress Rachel Roberts. Then, there was Hope, a fairly well-known American actress at that time. Hope had brought along her daughter to play with the Selznick child. Sam's wife and David's wife, the actress Jennifer Jones, were vacationing on the east coast. Nothing too exciting happened until the wine finally made its presence known in the mental distortions of the guests. Being a non-drinker, I observed the activities and saw what poor judgment was being exhibited. Rachel started complaining about her husband's lack of romantic competence, which she admitted she knew before marrying him. Her regrets surfaced for everyone to hear. Whining accompanied the wine, it seemed. Nothing was held back.

As the evening grew late, Hope decided to take her child and drive home. Nope! Even though I was very young and out of my element with this group, I stood up and said there would be no way that anyone, filled with alcohol, would take the child out on that particular road in the middle of the night. The child would have to stay. There began a war among the guests with abusive language and endless stupidity thrown around for an hour or so before Hope agreed to stay the night.

Steve Bochco was another interesting fellow who flitted in and out of my life when I was with Sam. Sam had hired Steve right out of Carnegie Melon University to help him learn the film business by reading scripts and working on concepts.

We were good buddies, nothing more. His office was right next to mine. Years later, Steve became a successful television producer and writer of several award-winning televisions series like *Hill Street Blues, L.A. Law, and NYPD Blue.*

My horizons expanded and my future was wide open.

Goodbye, my Father

The charcoal-broiled steak dinners finally caught up with my father and cancer set in. Treatment was rudimentary. After most of his stomach was removed, my mother finally called to inform me. I made trips home as often as possible, as did my brother. There was no way around the inevitable; my father became weaker and thinner. I knew he liked the thinner part. He'd been heavy his whole life. It probably came from associating food with security as a child. He protected himself by eating more than necessary. He often said that he wished he'd lived his whole life as a thinner person.

My father volunteered for experimental radiation treatment that caused deep burning with a severe pain he could not escape. He withstood it because he could take anything, but I couldn't. On my last visit to the hospital before he passed away, I walked into his room, turned and walked out. I couldn't bear to see him so diminished. It was a crushing realization that this one whom I loved so much and who had been my protector and supporter for so long was dying.

On his deathbed, my mother, my brother, and my father's brothers were present. I am told that he looked around and asked, "Where is Sally?"

My friend Jeanie knew where I was and in whose arms I was sleeping. Having moved out of his home, Sam had taken up residence at a popular Bel Air motel. Jeanie had her husband make the call. My father was gone and I was crushed.

As I drove north to Bakersfield, all I could think of was how glad I was that he'd played his last round of golf with me before he went into the hospital. It had been lovely to be together, even though I knew he was in pain. That evening, he sun was about to set before we went in for dinner. There would be no replacing my love for him.

Goodbye, my Love

My future was now wide open and I was in it now without my father. I suppose Sam might have been a father figure for me. Who knows? He was definitely a big help through this loss. But then I soon lost him as well.

All during my time with Sam, I needed to function in a presentable fashion in such elegant and sophisticated company. Fortunately, another friend came to my aid. Suzy Levinson was about my size, and she had a brother who owned a fine clothing company called California Girl. Every year he gifted Suzy with a sample of every dress in his new line and she in turn bestowed his previous year's line on me. My wardrobe was outstanding and nothing I could afford on a simple, secretary's salary. I was more than presentable.

One evening when I was in a less presentable state, lying on fluffy, blue comforters that Sam had given me, he rested his head on my chest. "Oh, my God!" he said, "Your heart is beating a hundred miles an hour." The next day he sent me to his doctor, who took a blood sample.

"I've never seen so much thyroid in anyone's blood in my life," he said. "What have you been doing?"

"I've been taking thyroid pills."

You can find a quack anywhere, if you are looking for one. And I had found one. For a price, he would write any crazy prescription you wanted. I had the strange idea that thyroid pills would keep me slim by revving up my metabolism (thin was the first requirement in fashion, as it still is today.) Supporting this rationale, I remembered hearing our friendly, family pharmacist in Bakersfield say that thyroid was something each person had to adjust for himself. That was the opening I needed to self-medicate with this hormone, popping thyroid tables whenever I felt the urge, sometimes four or five times a day.

"Well, stop it! Don't take a thing!" the doctor ordered, after I told him what I'd been doing.

Sam had saved my life.

No promises were ever made with this man. In fact, on our very first outing, Sam asked, "What do you want?"

"To love," I said, "and make memories." A perfect line to hand a married man.

Days turned into weeks, then month and years with me scurrying around, accommodating this man and his life, until we both moved in different directions; I was more or less pushed out. His was toward a new life with a new wife, but not me. I was heart-broken at this discovery – with it, sadness set in and I stumbled to try to find balance. Then, a new door opened that set me free.

*

A day without love is a day lost.

*

With two men I loved now out of my life, I had to check my heart for a new course.

13 A NEW KIND OF DANCE

An Expanding Life

Friends were always close by to lift me up when I needed it. My friends rallied to support me in this particular situation and helped me find a new direction.

One of these friends was Michael Tannenbaum, an attorney, originally from New York, who worked with country-western music legend Merle Haggard and singer/songwriter Paul Simon, among other musical stars. Michael needed to move Paul's music publishing operation out to California from New York where he could oversee it. He needed a "front" person, someone to "manage" Charing Cross Music Publishing, under his guidance, someone who would be a proper representative at BMI and ASCAP (performance rights organizations) functions, as well as keep an office tidy. He dangled this attractive managerial position over my head for months, until he finally bequeathed it on me. As I remember, my salary was $6,000 a year. With this, I could pay for an apartment, a car, gas, food, and go to any movie I wanted. My needs were small as were my wants.

My life at this point consisted of playing light-hearted, social tennis in and around Beverly Hills and Malibu on the weekends, and working during the week in a small office at the corner of Sunset Boulevard and Doheny Drive for Paul via Michael. The "work" was easy. I just opened letters with royalty checks for massive amounts of money gathered from music performance-rights organizations. I also opened letters with tiny amounts of money from school kids who wanted permission to use some of Paul's lyrics from *Bridge Over Troubled Waters* for their yearbooks. I answered the letters, granted permission to the kids and gave Michael all the money.

As I had a private office in which no one visited, I took the opportunity to start meditating and reading interesting books... spiritual books. Many I bought at the Bodhi Tree in West Hollywood, a beloved bookstore for the "in" people at the time that offered mysterious and otherworldly books, as well as a wide range of philosophical and spiritual books.

It was a time that, as young people, we drank herbal teas and ate huge vegetarian salads and nut-filled cookies at health food cafes on the Sunset Strip or Melrose Avenue while the traffic whizzed by. It was the time of the avant-garde musical *Hair*, The Beatles, and the influx of mind-altering drugs with the Vietnam War in the background.

Then, my friend Trudie Fator from my college days, told me that I needed to take a private session with a particular "dance-movement" therapist. She would not tell me what it was about, only that I had to do it. So, I did.

I made an appointment and showed up. I was game for most anything and at this point welcomed something new.

Joan Englander was a student of the great Mary Whitehouse, the creator of dance/movement therapy who headed up that department at UCLA.

Joan had a little dance studio that she rented off of Santa Monica Boulevard, at the edge of Beverly Hills. It had wooden floors and a long wall of mirrors with a ballet bar. The mirrors were draped so that you could not view yourself or see what you looked like as you moved. You had to "feel" the movement and not "think" it. It was moving from the inside without judgment and without preconceived ideas of how or what you should do. It revealed the fact that there was natural movement within every person that would show itself and animate that person if it were left to its own devices. This energy was pure and powerful, if one would only trust it and let go. It was movement beyond the rational mind. In other words, the person did not make the movement, the movement moved the person. It was something that was hard to explain, but was extraordinary to experience. It required "letting go." "Letting go" suited me just fine. I'd had years of controlled movement and was only now feeling free of this programming and the bonds of expectations.

Joan was a small woman in her early thirties, warm with a seriousness of purpose. Dressed in a leotard, she sat cross-legged on the floor with a couple of drums nearby in case she felt the need to add some rhythmic sound to match the movement a student might be doing. The movement in this way was creative, experiential, and set you free like nothing else. I loved it!

Joan was a great teacher, or rather facilitator, of this work – truly gifted. But, like many who were on their right path at one time, she felt the need to go off on a spiritual trip and ended up traipsing around India, following in the wake of the Roman Catholic nun Mother Teresa. This led to her ending up homeless and destitute, rejecting her own particular talent. What a shame. You really need to know your own calling and not hang on the robes of another. I didn't know mine at this point either. Working with Joan got me closer to it.

However, as much as I loved my sessions with Joan, there was one problem: I could not work on the floor. I could not sit on the floor. I could not move on the floor. I was thin beyond thin and to sit or move on the floor was excruciatingly painful.

Beyond thin and delightfully happy about it

Thin Beyond Thin

How did I get in this emaciated state? Well, like all young girls of my era, we had our role models and they were not the lovely, full-figured women of the forties and fifties that can be seen today in old movies on TCM. Our examples of feminine beauty were Twiggy and Audrey Hepburn. These were waif-like females who appeared too thin to care for themselves and needed men of substance to look after them. At this time, young women either married young and built a family or floundered around helplessly until some man saved them. This was a time long before feminism took hold, a time before women took hold of their own lives. So, we the young girls of our era, were programmed for thinness... the thinner, the better.

My particular route to this desired state came about through a series of efforts to reconfigure my healthy, balanced body with its appropriate curves to one in which there were no curves or recognizable girlish forms. It started in college; no bulimia for me, it was pills. Little by little, I became littler and littler.

Oh, how I wish we could examine our rationale for the efforts we make when we are in the middle of making them. What was really behind that desire to be super thin? Not just to emulate the role models of the day, but perhaps to attract the men. Men had to be strong, stronger than women, so women needed to be weak. That's what I think I did – became a weaker version of myself. I needed rescuing. What nonsense!

*

Dancing with the feet is one thing.

Dancing with the heart is another.

*

Dancing nourished my soul, but definitely not my body.

14 MORE HELP

My Mother's Answer

When my health was threatened, my mother stepped in. My mother was a woman of her times, a homebody with no great ambition except to be a good mother and care for her husband and home, which she did well. This meant a focus on healthy food and all things Gladys Lindberg recommended. Gladys was the original "health food nut" and had her own health food stores everywhere promoting her brand of health.

In my mother's search to bring order back to my physical body, she came across a popular book at one of Gladys' stores titled *Food is Your Best Medicine* by Dr. Henry Bieler. Bieler's claim to fame was that Gloria Swanson, a forties movie icon (i.e., *Sunset Boulevard*) was one of his long-time patients and swore by his "Bieler Broth."

This "broth" consisted of any squash you could find, with an emphasis on zucchini, plus celery and a variety of other green vegetables... and water. Occasionally you could dunk a small piece of meat into it. That was it.

My mother took me to Dr. Bieler. After a few tests, Dr.

Bieler discovered that my liver was a mess, evidently due to all of the pills that I had taken, and it needed to be cleared out. He prescribed the notorious Bieler Broth. It was to be consumed for a few weeks to do this cleansing.

The strange thing was that I liked this vegetable stew. It was easy to fix; I didn't have to think about what to eat, and it wouldn't add an ounce of fat to my already skinny frame. The problem was that I never went back to Dr. Bieler to see what the next step in his process was. He'd given me my perfect diet, or so it seemed.

That's how I ended up on Joan Englander's floor, expressing my discomfort.

Joan, in her wisdom, sent me to her natural healer, Dr. Giovanni Boni.

A Real Change

Among all the wise men that I had met or would meet in my life, Dr. Boni, was one of the wisest.

My interest in the spiritual aspect of life started long before... probably when someone gave me a copy of *The Prophet* by Kahlil Gibran.

There were, of course, visits to the Bodhi Tree bookstore. However, there was nothing in my past that congealed this vague interest in spiritual matters. There was no particular religious affiliation or belief system with which I resonated.

Yet, at this moment I landed in a heaven-like environment, the home and offices of Therese and Gianni

Boni.

On my first visit, I sat in a small room in a straight-back chair facing Dr. Boni at his desk, and took in the surroundings. The room was white, filled with fresh air with the hint of gardenia that glided in through a window from the garden. There were photographs of interesting people on the wall, a small pyramid on his desk along with a long, perfectly clear crystal stalactite, a variety of beautiful stones, and a tiny dish with gold needles. I wondered if these were for me.

Dr. Boni was an acupuncturist and homeopathic doctor from Italy. His name was passed secretly from one person to another in order to ensure his safety. Acupuncture was not understood and was therefore outlawed in the U.S. at that time. He worked under a chiropractic license.

He took my arm with his beautiful, soft hands, read the pulses on my wrist, and said, "Take off your shoes." I did as he requested. "Go to the beach in your mind," he said. In my imagination, I walked along the deep beachfront in Santa Monica, close to the water.

"Ouch!" I winced when he inserted a needle into the kidney point on my little toe.

"Go to the beach again," he repeated. The second little toe was attacked.

"Oooow!"

"You'd better jump in the water on this one," he said. With that, he thrust a needle right into the bottom of my foot, the heart point. I thought I would faint, the pain was so intense, and then it subsided.

We sat and waited while the needles did their work. Gianni had a kind face, a compassionate face with joy behind it. His eyes twinkled. One side of his face was distorted, enlarged, as if there were a small plate in it. He explained that an insect had stung him long ago and it had created this condition. He had been warned not to remove the tumor, as it would release poison into his body if it were pierced. He said that having this disfigurement reminded him to be more understanding of others who were deformed in some way. Compassion seemed to be his very essence.

I trusted him. I knew he could fix me... and I certainly needed fixing.

Therese Furino Boni

After some time, there was a knock on the door. It opened and his wife Therese stuck her head in. "Your next appointment is here, Gianni." She was stunning, as if she were right out of Egypt. She was actually Italian-French, but had the profile of Nefertiti. Her black hair had wisps of silver in the front that bounced over a high forehead and icy blue eyes. She was tall, maybe five-nine, but her particular presence, like my father's, made her seem even taller. She wore an outfit of blue denim, stylish for the seventies.

Later she told me that she'd stuck her head in the office to see who Gianni's new patient was. As she suspected, I was a mess.

I left with Dr. Boni's hand-written prescription for homeopathic remedies that I was to take to the Santa Monica Drug Company to fill.

Norman and Mary Litvak owned the Santa Monica Drug Company. It was a regular pharmacy until Dr. Boni set up his practice. He arranged to have the Livaks carry the homeopathic remedies he needed for his patients. These remedies were unheard of in every other pharmacy, except perhaps Khiel's in New York. Strangely, Norman and Mary Litvak and Gianni all had the same birthday, March 15th, the Ides of March.

Santa Monica Drug was originally a modest, little establishment on a side street until homeopathy became understood and accepted. Now the pharmacy has become a thriving business and has moved to a grander location, and is considered the authority on all things homeopathic. Norman and Mary's grandson and family now run it. A picture of Dr. Boni hangs on one wall.

Weekly treatments from Gianni sent me to this pharmacy regularly. During one of these treatments, I asked Gianni how he became an acupuncturist. He said that many years before, in Italy, Therese, his wife, was working for a well-known German acupuncturist. Many young people would ask this doctor if he would train them. No, he would never take on a student. Then, one night Therese became paralyzed. She couldn't move at all and Gianni went into a trance and treated her with his hands. The next morning, she was fine. When she told the German doctor about this, he said, "Bring Gianni to me. I will work with him." It was because Gianni already knew… he already had the knowledge.

A Permanent Guest

I was also becoming a regular guest in the Boni's home. Therese, who was equally fascinating as her husband, had her own business in their home too, that of teaching languages. While still in Italy, she developed a unique method for teaching languages involving movement. This she taught to a number of people in the West L.A./Beverly Hills area who came to her home-studio for classes. Some days it would be French, some days Italian or Spanish, and there was even a bit of dabbling in Russian on special occasions. Everyone loved her. You couldn't help it; she was dynamic, dramatic, magnetic, and strikingly beautiful. On top of that, she was wise, deeply wise, and cooked like a pro. Anyone who was in this home at mealtime was welcome to sit down and join in. I was one.

However, as tasty as this Italian food was, I still adhered to my diet of huge stew pots full of squash, and only sampled Therese's fare.

Slowly I improved, but I was still rail thin. Somehow Gianni's treatments cleared areas in my consciousness that allowed beneficial and prophetic dreams to come through. In one such dream I was with some folks up in the sky. We seemed to be just sitting there, looking around at the billowy, white clouds when I noticed that we were not in a plane. I became startled and confused until I heard a voice say, "Leave your rational mind behind." Yes, I was learning that the rational mind had limits, and life had delightful surprises if you could get beyond ordinary thinking.

Another dream ended with a bang that sent my then boyfriend running stark naked into the street. He soon ran squealing out of my life as well. The list of boyfriends faded. There had been a film writer, a fight promoter, an attorney or two, a football player, a game show creator, a tennis champion, a racecar driver, and an artist. All gone. This life disappeared as my interest in spiritual matters expanded. This was love on a higher, grander scale.

*

Fall in love with life. Life is already in love with you.

*

It is amazing how mirror-like life is, I found. The more I jumped into life with my whole heart, the more it reciprocated.

15 BACK ON THE COURT

Moving Outside

I continued to "manage" the music publishing company with one hand, but then began to explore teaching tennis with the other. Then another dream showed me living fulltime on a tennis court. It was the combination of the dance-movement work and being with the Bonis that prompted me to make the shift to teaching tennis full time. I did it slowly at first; covering myself in case I couldn't make rent money. But once I got into it, I knew I would be fine.

I often played social tennis at the home of Jennings and Monica Lang in Beverly Hills. Jennings was the head of television film production at Universal Studios and a longtime mover and shaker in the Hollywood scene. He had produced many major motion pictures on his own, including *Play Misty for Me* with Clint Eastwood. It was a beautiful, spacious estate on Mountain Drive, only a hop and a skip from my office. I loved to play there and I was delighted when the Langs offered to let me use their court to teach on.

I quickly got an answering service to take calls at the

office (there were no cell phones at that time) so that I could pop over to the Lang's court to give a lesson.

Jennings Lang at play

Therese was my first student. She jumped into it totally because it was much like her language lessons: learning with movement (in my case, "movement from the inside") in a natural, non-programmed way. I could never teach how I had been taught – rigid strokes and preconceived ideas about where to hit the ball. The motions I worked with were natural to each person and contained movements that were universal to everyone… throwing, twirling, blocking, chopping… and always totally relaxed, except for the blocking and chopping. I incorporated the Zen philosophy I was studying by redirecting a student's focus to the enjoyment of the movements and play, like dancing, and away from the results. It was a new way of playing; it was freeing and the most fun you could have on a tennis court. And the results, although not the focus of the instruction, were always better in the end. Everyone loved it… especially creative people.

What I learned about movement was mind-boggling. Freeing a person in his or her physical actions freed that person in ways that affected their whole life. It did mine for sure. It made me happier and lighter in every way. "Freedom" was the key word – doing what the moment dictated in your movement, not hanging onto predetermined patterns. It was "letting go" in a big way... trusting yourself and life. That's when I think I became "fearless," trusting and therefore fearless.

Jennings sent me many students, many from the entertainment industry... actresses Jill St. John and Valerie Perrine, director Milos Forman, singer Barbra Streisand, Swedish actress Bibbi Anderson, songwriter Marilyn Bergman, singer Helen Reddy, and some of the Lloyd Bridges clan. These folks sent other folks, and I was in business – and out of the music-publishing world.

Spreading Happy Tennis

I wanted to be outdoors and not be cooped up in an office ever again. My teaching expanded to Malibu and The Colony there. Show business folks like Joel Grey, Larry and Mai Hagman, Jack Warden, William Mankiewicz were added to my list of students, plus a bunch of kids who belonged to the grand beachfront homes there. I was very comfortable with this crowd and knew that I could help each person by getting him or her to relax, which released a ton of energy. I seemed to be able to see inside a person, see the blocks and then come up with a way to free them in movement. This ability to see inner movement in this way, might have come from my art class days when I could see the essence of a model's pose and put it down in seconds. Everything was revealed on a tennis court... a person's need to control or their ability to be flexible, a person's materialistic nature by his or her attachment to results or a person's aesthetic nature by their enjoyment of the movement around the court. It was really fun. I didn't talk much, just showed someone something and let the person discover what that would do. No, not many words. It was tennis beyond the rational mind – feeling tennis, Zen tennis.

That's the way I played now and that's the way I taught. In The Colony I was so brazen that I often wore a bikini when I taught so that I could go for a dip in the ocean between lessons.

For years this little one-mile strip of land in Malibu called The Colony, that runs parallel to Coast Highway along the beach, had been a slice of country life for the ultra-wealthy and entertainment giants. Behind the guardhouse, there was a drive, an alley really, that separated the homes on the beachfront from a few tennis courts and the less desirable homes on the east side of the lane. And, it was the access to these courts that was the cause of more rumblings and arguments than the actors who lived there had ever played in films. Some of the residents owned a court outright; others only owned a portion of a court. All courts were locked and required keys to enter. The local hardware store did a big business duplicating keys for those who didn't have legal access to a court yet got their hands on a key.

I was allowed keys to all the courts. I would just arrive, pop into one of the homes, snag a key, jump on a court and start teaching. People would stop by the court and set up a time for their lesson. I was booked all day long. Exhausting, but fun.

*

Happy days are made by happy people.

Happy people are made by choice!

*

It seemed that the happier I got, the happier I got.

16 SOCIAL TENNIS

Palm Springs Outings

Not only did I teach tennis on these beautiful courts with the salty ocean air rolling through them, I played a bit of social doubles with some of the residents. Occasionally I would join them on their outings. One in particular was to play in the member-only Palm Springs Racquet Club Pabst Blue Ribbon Tournament at the outskirts of windy, sunny Palm Springs.

The Racquet Club and Palm Springs held a special place in my heart. I had been there with my parents when I was a young, budding player. It was magical then. The air was divine when the wind wasn't blowing. A small area of grass and flowers separated the two main courts where you could sit and kibitz with all sorts of interesting characters, and they were characters.

The Club's beloved tennis hostess and tournament director, Julie Copeland, would send us onto the courts during the day, and the famous Bamboo Lounge (where it is said that the original "bloody Mary" was created) would draw us inside in the evening.

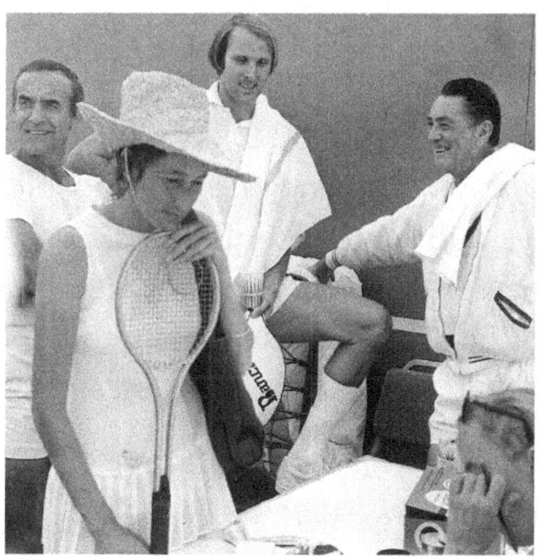

Julie Copeland at the tournament desk with Ricardo Montablan, basketball giant Rick Barry, and Macdonald Carey

The Racquet Club had a notorious history. Old-time actors Charlie Farrell and Ralph Bellamy founded it way back in the thirties. It was the party venue and safe haven for much of Hollywood's show business elite for their dalliances. Four of the bar stools had reserved plaques on them for Clark Gable, Charles Farrell, William Powell, and Spencer Tracy. At the time that I frequented the Racquet Club, you could find the Hungarian actress and socialite ZaZa Gabor, her mother, and sisters holding court in the dining room. Or, you could watch singer Dinah Shore scampering around a tennis court while TV actor James Garner was trying to do the same. Zeppo Marx, of the comic Marx Brothers family, would be keeping his eye on his wife Barbara who had her eye on Frank Sinatra. There was old money, the Hiltons and the Kennedys; and new money Bob Evans, head of Paramount Pictures, who was perpetually escorting one of his many wives there or looking for another. The place was filled with high jinks and high-profile patrons.

On Sunday morning, the last day of the tournament, I was feeling exceedingly exuberant having danced the night away to the tunes of Sammy Cahn. Sammy had taken over the piano from one of the band members to play some of his many hit tunes and the dance floor was cleared for just my partner and me. I flew around the floor and through the air, no definable steps just moving where the music took me. What a delight!

That sense of flying remained with me the next morning. Not having reached a reasonable state of balance in my life as yet, I jumped around my bungalow wildly. My leg caught the edge of a table, lifting a layer of skin the length of my lower right leg. I put a towel over it and pronounced some healing words, but that did nothing; it had to be stitched.

A cosmetic surgeon was brought into the emergency room at the Palm Springs hospital to do the work. He took his time and warned me, "This skin is very thin and the stiches are tiny and fragile. You must be very careful and not move your leg or it will tear."

I was not only out of the tournament; I was out of life. Moving was everything to me. Alas, one of my fellow tennis friends helped by taking me home with him, then feeding and caring for me for a couple of days before it was safe for me to move around on my own on crutches. He was working on the script for *One Flew Over the Cuckoo's Nest* and would ask, "What would Nurse Ratched say here? 'Aren't you ashamed?' or 'You should be ashamed.'" Gad, I didn't know, but he must have gotten it right because he won an Academy Award that year for his contribution to the film.

Once I was in my own apartment again, I could at least do a little writing and artwork, but not move... until one night. It was like a dream, but not exactly. It was kind of an out-of-body experience in which I was taken by the hand and began flying around my apartment, bouncing off of the walls, flying in one direction and then flying in the other. Back and forth I soared, never touching the floor. It was so much fun and such a thrill; I knew that those who gave me this experience must have known how much I missed moving. They had come to give me this escape. What a treat! It felt wonderful and I was grateful for this visit.

I had had this feeling before when jumping or hitting the ball and knew it must somehow be connected to moving in the ethers. (I think that's how Michael Jordan could hang in the air. He was moving in his etheric body.) Occasionally one of my students would experience this weightless motion during a lesson. The ball would sail off their racket at tremendous speed and they'd say, "I hardly felt it. There was no effort." In Zen, the saying is: "It happened." Still, it was not quite the same thing as flying around my bedroom!

My leg healed beautifully. I sent the doctor a hand-painted card that said, "Doctors with patience always have patients." He had taken great patience with my leg and it paid off. Not a trace of that incident remained, only the memory of my sailing through the air.

Playing with the Kennedys

Another trip to the Racquet Club in the desert and another court assignment by Julie Copeland had me playing doubles with Senator Robert Kennedy and his wife Ethel. They were obviously tenacious competitors and the good senator chided me when I aced him, "Okay, we know you can do that. Now let's play." I pulled back and continued in a manner to make the match enjoyable for everyone. "Customer tennis," it was called.

George Stevens, Jr., Sally, Senator Robert Kennedy and his wife Ethel after tennis at the Palm Springs Racquet Club. What is my stance revealing?

After tennis, they invited me to join them for a swim and lunch at actor Robert Stack's home where they were staying. Actress Shirley MacLaine and Senator John Tunney joined the party and it was Tunney who received the chiding this time for not having voted in favor of a pet project of the Senator. The atmosphere was light-hearted and Senator Kennedy was as playful as rumored, pinching me on the bottom as he swam underwater. I can still see him flipping his lock of hair back with his hand and warming everyone with his smile. Everyone called him "Bobby."

*

Fun requires a little dance music.

*

Where dancing led me, I cannot say, but it was always fun.

17 AN EXPANDING SPIRIT

More Studying, More Learning, More Meaning

Another dream, another change. This dream had a strong message: in it a voice said, "There is no spiritual growth on drugs." I never touched marijuana again. It was a part of every young, hip person's life in the L.A. area, but no longer for me. It started as a lark, just an amusing thing to do like having a glass of wine.

Boy, I learned to take these messages seriously. On a couple of occasions, I hadn't and paid the price. Although we young people just thought using marijuana was fun and harmless, evidently it wasn't. I was now aware of the fact that we were all on a spiritual path, whether we knew it or not. And, for growth in this area, it wasn't enough to go on in the same old ordinary way; you had to make an effort. You had to make changes. You had to be conscious of your actions and interactions with others and the affects your choices would have. And if you learned something important, you had to put it into practice... just like learning tennis. So, if drugs were off limits, there would be no more drugs for me. Later I'd find out why.

The more that I studied spiritual matters and spent time with the Bonis, the richer my life became.

During one of my hanging-around days at their home, Therese discovered that I could draw, that I even had a degree in Fine Art from USC. This led to my illustrating many of her language lessons. I would just draw some very simple characters to augment the text in her lessons. It was not much really; however, she was so encouraged she wanted to know what else I could draw. "Figures," I said. "Nude figures." With that she took off her clothes right there in the living room and posed nude for me.

While I was preparing my drawing paraphernalia, there was a knock on the front door. It was the actor Yul Brynner, star of the Broadway show and film *The King and* I, arriving for his treatment with Gianni. Therese grabbed a shawl to hold in front of her as he walked past. Then he stopped, bowed toward us in the style of the King of Siam and said, "Ladies, please carry on."

During these early times with the Bonis, I was led to read the books by Joan Grant about her past lives, the Zen books of Hagel and Alan Watts, Elizabeth Haich's beautiful book *Initiation*, and books about the lives of Ramana Maharshi and other saints. I was absorbed by these books and could sense the depth of the truths they disclosed.

An Extraordinary Master

I read; I taught tennis; I ate squash; and I returned to this magical home often. There was no end to the interesting people who passed through it. It seemed to be a magnet for extraordinary and spiritually aware people. I became a fixture there, like a fly on the wall, absorbing everything and not making a peep. The visitor list included the high mucky muck astrologers from Sedona, the tremendously gifted Sufi from England Richard Field, the yoga master Georg Feuerstein, and the Boni's close friend Kathryn Walsh, a renowned clairvoyant. Then there was Michael Malosek, a swami and spiritual master, who had spent thirty days in silence in the caves of Arunachala, India with the great 20th century Indian saint, Ramana Maharshi. Michael had remained in India with Ramana for four years.

The Master Michael Malosek

I had known a few wise people and intelligent people in my short life, but a spiritual master, like Michael, was someone beyond my limited experience and understanding. Yet, I knew by the reverence with which the Bonis held for Michael that he was indeed an extraordinary human being. By keeping my eyes and ears open, I did come to understand that such a person is one who is dedicated to the truth and upholds the universal laws and principles, is in complete control of his inner state, is free of the personality's dictates and limitations, and is motivated by unselfish love. And too, his consciousness is without bounds and his interest is only in fulfilling the Divine Will. An exceptional being of this degree of evolvement is almost inconceivable to fathom by ordinary people, even when he walks among us. I was blessed to be in his presence.

Michael was in his eighties when I met him, and lived as the guest of Antonia Vidor, daughter of the early film giant King Vidor. She was the owner of a horse ranch in the Malibu hills. She was on a spiritual awareness path herself and provided a private suite for Michael where he could play his cello, receive visitors now and then, and do his work. He was a musical genius and played in the New York Philharmonic Orchestra at sixteen. Also, while getting his doctorate in medicine at Columbia during the day, he played in the New York City Opera Company at night. On top of that, he performed a dominant role in the music for the 1940 Disney film *Fantasia*.

Michael walked two miles every day, ate pure food, and did his most important work at night… that of prayer and harmonizing the energies of the planet. How little we know of what goes on in our behalf by higher beings such as Michael.

Michael was not here so much as a teacher or healer, as other self-realized masters are; his work was different. He, of course, did teach when you were in his presence, and he could also heal. And, he was tremendously powerful. He told me about an incident that occurred when he was a young man. A pack of wolves came upon him while he was walking in the forest near his village in Czechoslovakia. He explained how he held them off with his will. He had to stay fixed in one place for a very long time, and with tremendous force and focus he was able to save his life. Yes, he was very powerful.

Michael's eyes were as blue as the sky on a clear day and they looked right through you. The lines on his hand formed a star, the sign of a mystic. Therese called Michael the Master of Purity. We all learned from him the value of maintaining the physical body in its purest state. As he said, "You have to keep the glass of the lantern clean so that the light may shine through."

An Initiation

The first time the Bonis took me to visit Michael, I had a short, private audience with him. During it he asked me the ultimate question, "Do you will to do good?"

This was nothing I had ever thought about, then without any hesitation, I answered, "Yes." It was a kind of initiation, I realized later. I have often thought of that statement and what it meant. It was a "life-changing" or perhaps a life-directing statement that affected everything I would do in life and the choices I would make from then on. It was so simple, yet infinitely meaningful. It doesn't mean that everything I did after that was "good to the last drop." It certainly set my intention on the right side of every choice I would make.

"Do you will to do good?" To say, "Yes" is better than a salute to the flag or a Girl Scout pledge. It is an essential declaration. How I wish this idea of goodness and doing good was re-established in our culture. I have the oddest feeling that many young people today are confused about what is good. They don't understand that goodness is crucial to their own lives and that of others. The images young people see in films and on screens, and the outlandish lyrics of many songs have distorted their natural knowing. Goodness matters for goodness' sake!

There was another "aha" moment that I remember distinctly. Michael held up his hand and moved his little finger. "Without the will of God," he said, "we could not even do this." This was a humbling realization.

Off and on I would visit Michael on my own. It was never less than enlightening and oftentimes scary. His look would go right through you and if you had something hidden, he'd find it and straighten you out. No sweet hand-holding with someone like this. Masters are tough. They don't care about hurting your feelings. They are only interested in the truth.

There was one of these hidden somethings that he must have found within me because he gave me one of the most important pieces of advice anyone has ever given me. "Fall in love with Sally," he said. He knew that everything stemmed from there. Was it possible that I held some self-resentment? Had I let others down here and there? My parents? Maybe myself? I went to work on this idea, talking to myself and heaping love all over me.

I came to understand that falling in love with "yourself," in this case, "myself," meant that you were in love with the whole… everyone and everything. To clarify what he was implying: there is no "self" outside of yourself. So, that's what I did, I fell in love with me.

On one of my walks with Michael into the Malibu hills, we came upon a spot that had a tree branch that reached out over a creek. There was a rough, old rope with a bunch of knots on it tied to the branch. The girl who was walking with us was far braver than me. She grabbed the rope, wrapped her legs around it, sat on the knots and swung back and forth over the creek. It looked like fun, but I was hesitant. Michael insisted, "Trust yourself!" Fear was nothing he would tolerate. You handled what was before you. Okay, I did it and it was fun.

At one point, I was becoming too wrapped up in the spiritual books I was reading, especially the one about Ramana Maharshi's life. Even though Michael had the greatest respect for Ramana and loved him dearly, he came to me in a dream and told me to throw that book in the ocean. What he meant was: just live your own life. Don't imitate someone else's. Again, he was saying, "Rely on yourself."

This was somewhat of a theme, a tendency I had – of questioning myself. I would almost trust someone else's point of view over my own. Was this another remnant of being so programmed by my coach or my father during my tennis days – taking instruction endlessly? I really don't think I thought about much of anything meaningful until I met the Bonis.

Another Master

During the many visits with Therese and Gianni, I learned bits and pieces of their history. They told their stories, not to impress anyone, but to merely share their experiences and reveal truths. Nothing ordinary happened to them. Nothing prosaic surfaced. Their stories were better than any movie I had ever seen.

Therese and Dr. Giovanni Boni

Both Therese and Gianni were Italian and, in their youth, they were part of a group that studied under an extraordinary spiritual initiate by the name of Toddi. Toddi was a mathematician, also an Orientalist who spoke fourteen languages, taught at the University in Rome at the age of nineteen, wrote and edited numerous humor magazines, and was the author of many books, including *The Mathematical Explanation for the Non-Existence of Death*. The tales about

Toddi that each of them told were mind-boggling to me at first. However, I was getting used to having an open mind and not being surprised by anything I heard.

Much of the works by Toddi were banned and ultimately destroyed due to the Church's opposition to his philosophical points of view. This was common at that time. Anything esoteric or mystical was denounced.

Pietro Silvio Rivetta, known as Toddi

The first time Therese met Toddi she was seventeen and he was in his early fifties. She had heard him speak in an open forum and knew he had answers to many of the questions she had about life. So, she went to his studio, knocked on the door, and insisted that he meet with her. She wore a school-girlish frock, not too sophisticated; he was dressed in an elegant dark Chinese silk kimono. He peered at her through his monocle. After being invited in, she looked around at all the unusual things that filled the room. Then, he asked her what she was interested in. She answered, "Languages." She wanted to be a language teacher. With that, he asked her to get on top of an armoire he had in the room; he didn't tell her how or why. So, she moved a table over to the armoire, pushed a chair up to the table, climbed on the chair, then onto the table; put the chair on top of the table and used it to climb on top of the armoire. As she looked around, he asked, "What do you see?"

"Well," she said. "It looks very different from here."

"Yes," he said. "That's what another language is: a different point of view." She never forgot it. Perhaps that's what each person's experience is... a different point of view.

The stories about Toddi were still alive in both Gianni and Therese by the time I met them, but most especially in Therese. She truly loved him. These stories dotted in and out of conversations as examples of truths that she would be explaining to one us. There were more hangers-on than just me, you see... and we were all Geminis. Geminis it seemed love the company of other Geminis and Therese was one too. Gianni on the other hand was a Pisces who was happiest in the company of Geminis. All so convenient. The group consisted of Claire, a Swiss miss who taught languages at Loyola University; Diane, a gorgeous, New York high-fashion model; and Espy, a will-of-the-wisp girl; and me. We were all there for some type of healing and all were learning about life in the process.

At a later time in Therese's history with Toddi, she became his secretary at the university. He could change time and space and would often delay a mild heart attack that would occur during one of his lectures until he returned to his office to experience it. (He had been a smoker in his youth and the smoking had damaged his heart.)

In keeping with his Oriental nature, Toddi was also adept at origami. He carried a small pair of scissors and a few pieces of paper with him at all times. On one occasion, Therese accompanied Toddi on a bus trip. As she looked out the window, she saw the rain beginning to fall. Her expression clouded with the weather. "What is wrong?" he asked.

"I have a new coat and I don't want it to be ruined by the rain." With that Toddi pulled out his scissors, cut an image of the sun from a piece of paper, then stuck it on the window. As Therese reminisced, "It was magical; the rain stopped, the clouds parted, and the sun came out."

My favorite Toddi story was about the night that Toddi died. Therese was walking with him back from a lecture he had given when he announced that it was now his time. She ushered him upstairs to her apartment. He bathed and dressed himself saying that it would be easier for this to be done now rather than after. Next, he sat down in a soft armchair and asked for a little something sweet to drink. She mixed a demi-spoonful of jam into a tiny glass of water. He took a sip and closed his own eyes. As he began to drift off, he described his passing, "It's just as I have always told you, Kappy (his nickname for her.) There is no difference between this world and the next." Then, he smiled and said, "Wonderful. Wonderful. Wonderful." With each word his smile broadened and his expression became more beautiful.

She checked his pulse to confirm that he was gone. Without thinking, Therese took a sip from the same glass herself and fell into a state of bliss, samadhi.

From that moment on, after hearing this story, I was no longer afraid of death.

I continued to improve with Gianni's treatments and a special concoction Michael taught me to make. It was a cheese made from raw milk that had been curdled with lemon juice and strained through a cloth. It was so delicious and my body was so starved for nourishment that I consumed great quantities of it, too much of it, unbalancing my system once again.

*

A significant other is anyone in your presence.

*

Still, some seemed more significant than others.

18 MORE UPS AND DOWN

Pebble Beach Junket

Among my tennis students in Malibu, was a great character who was also a great character actor named Jack Ging. Ging was an intense, charging, muscular, alpha male with an extraordinarily sweet heart. We had fun on the tennis court with me trying to teach him how to relax and "go with the flow," and him trying to "slam bam, win the point as fast as you can." He was all push, push, shove, shove. He was eager and wanted to win, whatever the game.

That particular year, Ging had won the prestigious Bing Crosby Pro-Am Golf Tournament in Pebble Beach and now had his sights set on winning Clint Eastwood's Pro-Am Tennis Tournament, also to be held at Pebble Beach.

He invited me to be his partner. He and his wife Gretchen would fly me up on Friday for the weekend. I agreed and arrived in my usual laid-back garb of jeans and T-shirts from the Goodwill; this applied to the tennis court as well. I had long since given up the image of a Teddy Tinling model. I seemed to want to distance myself from the idea of being a regular tennis player. I was on the court now as a free spirit with a racket, moving uninhibitedly, spontaneously, yet powerfully, letting the results take care of themselves. It was a lovely way to play and to live.

Teaching days, happy but too thin

After a practice round at Pebble Beach, the Gings delivered me to Clint Eastwood's home where I was scheduled to stay during the event. Jack and Clint were big buddies and business partners in a dive in Redondo Beach and had shared the screen on more than one occasion (*Play Misty for Me* and *High Plains Drifter*.)

Maggie Eastwood had just given birth to baby Alison and was attending to her most of the time. I was delighted to be in this rambling, spacious home on the Monterey peninsula and even more delighted to find a carton of raw milk and a lemon or two in the refrigerator. A breakfast the next morning of my new favorite food, Michael's cheese, and I was ready to play. Later, when Maggie learned that the quart of raw milk was gone, she panicked. It was the last raw milk available in the area until Monday. She had it earmarked for their young son Kyle. As upset as she was, I wasn't. Nothing seemed to faze me. It was as if I were operating on a different plain, floating above my surroundings.

Ging grounded me. He was up for the challenge, determined to win the tournament. My job was to settle him down so that he would hit the ball in the court and then move over to make room for me to play the point. We muddled through the tournament and realized his dream of winning both Pebble Beach Pro-Ams in one year, an accomplishment that has never been repeated.

With tennis friends: lyricist Alan Bergman, a Pebble Beach club member and Lloyd Bridges at Clint's event

Like most pro-am events, a gala was held on the last evening with all the stars performing in some way – some sang songs, some told jokes. The ballroom was filled with the local, social set of Carmel and Pebble Beach, along with the visiting celebrities like the Smothers Brothers comedy team, John Wayne accompanying his wife Pilar, Bill Cosby, one of the Crosby boys, actor George Peppard, underwater TV star Lloyd Bridges, lyricist Alan Bergman, actor Ricardo Montalban, and others. I sat between television personality Merv Griffin and Clint at the dinner table, dressed in my favorite Indian gauze long dress… the same one that I had worn that morning at breakfast. When I danced with Clint, he told me that he was now meditating and taking long walks in the woods. A spiritual side of him was beginning to develop, he felt.

During this event, Merv talked to me about my different approach to tennis and suggested that I write a book about it and he would guarantee that his friend at Harcourt, Brace would publish it. It sounded good to me. I already had a draft started.

Returning to L.A, I learned that Jack Ging and Gretchen were fanatical country-western fans. I thanked them for a lovely time in Pebble Beach and gave them my entire collection of Merle Haggard albums, none of which I had ever listened to or even opened. The records had been a gift from Michael Tannenbaum, probably for carrying out a mission in his name for Merle. Merle had wanted a certain fiddle and as an efficient researcher, I tracked down the fiddle in a little shop in the Valley that specialized in unique guitars and violins. Once found, Merle decided he wanted two. I negotiated the price without revealing the buyer. I wiggled out a nice discount for the two instruments. On returning to the office with the fiddles, I vowed that I would never do that again… never take advantage of someone like the owner of this little shop for someone who could easily pay the full price and more. Merle was worth millions. I hoped he enjoyed the fiddles.

Beginnings of Writing and Illustrating

Zora's was a wonderful art supply store in Brentwood; it was around the corner from where I now lived. I would walk there and lose myself in the contents of this small shop. I was at home there as much as my coach George had been in a hardware store. Everything Zora had was the best of any art supply you could want. It was crammed with everything for creating anything. Besides the brushes and pencils that I liked, there were big, beautiful, yellow sketchbooks perfect for writing down thoughts and scribbling images. I bought them by the dozens and started filling them.

The Bonis continued their work. I continued my eavesdropping by stopping by after a day of teaching and joined the evening festivities. At one point, the party's honoree was the renowned English Sufi Richard Field who told us all about his group in England and about a particular meditation that they practiced. Every morning each Sufi, with closed eyes, would dive into their heart center and kind of flip around like a somersault and when he or she would open their eyes they would see life through their heart. It was easier to do than explain. It was as if the whole of creation was in each person's heart. It fascinated me, as I was definitely a heart person. I practiced this meditation to my own heart's delight.

Then, he told how each member wrote little stories to describe a realization or an awakening that he or she might have had. The idea of such a story was to share an understanding. This struck me as something I could do, especially with those yellow sketchbooks from Zora's.

Thus, I began. My apartment was all white, pristine in every way, with windows on the east side of the bedroom. Sunlight filled it, which bathed me as I awakened every morning. I kept a yellow sketchbook next to the bed and a pen ready for action. Before becoming fully conscious, I would meditate on a theme… something grand like unity, or harmony, that would then roll out like a little film. The film would not be in words, but more as images with feelings that evoked the words that went with them.

As soon as I would come back to ordinary consciousness, I would write it down. I'd write the story with some sketchy illustrations to go with it and later illustrate it on small pages with watercolors and pen and ink. That wasn't all. Next, with a self-made contraption, I would bind the pages into a book… a small book for children with a blue or yellow or pink cover. Lastly, I would place it carefully in a box for safekeeping. These were my treasures. These were messages that came to me… that were beyond what my simple mind could make up. I was tickled every time I went through this process. I learned something and perhaps one day others would read these stories and discover something themselves. All I can say about this is that it was like cooking something that I knew was good and special, and I couldn't wait for someone else to taste it. These stories were food for thought. They were mine but not entirely mine. Little by little, these books filled the box.

Learning Still

I continued my efforts to improve my health and at the same time learn about various healing modalities. I did this with Gianni. There was healing with translucent colored sheets of plastic and lights, one with Bach drops, and another with gemstones. I got my hands on a bunch of those small liquor bottles offered on airplanes. We needed the ones with vodka. Vodka I got. We needed a pearl, a sapphire, a diamond, a ruby, and more.

An old boyfriend of mine had a closet in his apartment that he never opened. It was filled with useful items. It was there that I found the vodka bottles. He didn't seem to mind if I poked around in it; so, I did. Along with those bottles, I found a ring that had most every gemstone we needed. This was my non-materialistic phase, so I saw that ring as simply a source of material for healing, not as a piece of jewelry. The boyfriend didn't care. So, I just popped the stones out of the ring and into the vodka bottles. Gianni and I placed them in the sun and voila we had a whole line of very powerful tinctures of the essences of these gems. These bottles became the mother tinctures. A couple of drops could be taken from these, diluted and placed under the tongue of someone who could use that particular energy. Gianni knew who needed what.

Because Michael emphasized purity so much, I went to great lengths to purify my body too. There was a well-known liver cleanse at the time that required drinking nearly a quart of olive oil along with the juice of six lemons. Why not? I would try most anything. What a mistake!

I turned yellow, and it took Gianni about ten treatments with painful needling to get my liver to understand that I was not trying to kill myself. I apologized to Gianni and my liver and would try to do better.

Major Mistake

I was still fragile, but improving. Then, I made a tragic, novice's mistake. I began experimenting during meditation with raising the Kundalini (that most powerful divine energy located at the base of the spine.) The problem was that I did not fully understand what I was doing. This activity happened over a period of several days and the effects were certainly blissful and addictive. I took meditating to new heights for me, entering intoxicating states of consciousness for which I had no support and no protection. With the inevitable fall from this elevated state, I ended up in a trance, will-less and motionless for days. This Kundalini work, I later learned, was something that no one should ever undertake alone or without proper guidance. The energy that was released required a very strong physical structure to withstand the intensity of the vibration and prevent damage to certain centers in the body, especially the brain. Obviously, I did not have that structure.

It was Therese and Claire who realized that something was wrong, came to my door and broke into my apartment. They gathered me up and took me back to the Bonis to stay and heal.

As Therese said later, "If anybody else had found you, you would have ended up in an insane asylum."

They cared for me, fed me, watched over me and tried to keep me from making any more disastrous, wrong steps. Gianni used the needles too with sessions every day.

There was no popping back from this situation; I could barely walk. I ate whatever Therese fixed which had to be mild and Gianni tended to my mental state, explaining that "discernment" was essential when meditating and hearing voices. I had gotten into such a weakened state that the sheaths that separated my everyday hearing from the voices on the other side had nearly disappeared. I learned that "discernment" was one of the tests on the spiritual path. I had failed miserably. It is one thing to be carefree and another thing to be careless. I had been dangerously careless.

So now I not only prayed hard for healing and balance, but I needed to pay attention to what I heard inwardly. Gianni insisted that I always ask where a voice came from if I heard something "other worldly" by demanding, "Identify yourself; who are you?"

Then in the kindest way, Gianni softened my saddened heart... believe me, I was heartsick over having taken such a wrong step... he said, "Don't worry. They (meaning the voices) don't bother with just anybody. You must be destined to do something important." Evidently my ego needed a little boosting.

Gianni also explained that probably my previous drug use had left openings in my subtle bodies that allowed these attachments to take hold. So, here it was – the real danger of drug use. Under the influence of drugs, a person's will tended to be put into a passive state which could leave that person open and vulnerable, in other words – will-less. I could see that now. It made perfect sense to me. I'd experienced it – this passive state. It is considered the most detrimental state for any person to be in. A person who is in a negative state will eventually see their error and make a change. At least they are in action. But a passive person is not operating at all.

Later when I tried sharing this information with others, I found it not to be so easy. It didn't seem to be enough to tell someone that drug use was unwise. The "Just say No" campaigns didn't work. Young people wanted to make their own mistakes. I'd have to think about this and eventually an idea did come to me much later… a way to plant this idea, the danger of drug use, in a book for young children.

As bad as I ended up after this "episode," during it I experienced the greatest joy and the profound realization that all things, everything and all beings, every single one was alive and united, no matter how separate they might appear. It was a knowing that has never left me. And it was a knowing that has affected how I touched, held, spoke to or listened to anything or anyone from then on, including myself. It was a different point of view.

And too, as troubling as any state that someone might be in who came into the Boni's home, there was always a sparkle, a tickle in the air. It was nourishing and delightful, and whatever anyone might have done or the shape they might be in, it was never so serious as to be beyond hope. There was fun in everything and laughter to go with it. Most fittingly, Therese wore the fragrance JOY by Jean Patou. It was her fragrance; it was her essence.

I was following Gianni's orders now and earnestly made an effort to right myself when another interesting dream showed up. In this one, a voice told me that I must be very still. I checked; the voice was authentic. Then I was taken out of my body and a group of people worked on it. Once they put me back, I awakened.

Later that day, I realized that I was better; I had more energy. When Gianni noticed this, I told him about my dream. He said, "That was not a dream; that was a healing."

Achilles Heel

Not long after that, as Gianni and I sat together one afternoon waiting for the needles to work, he asked, "What do you think your Achilles heel is?"

I had never thought about this. I never realized that I had one.

"I don't know," I said.

"Extremism," he answered. "In everything you do, you overdo. You go too far. You do too much."

He was right, of course. Whatever I ate, I ate too much, or I didn't eat at all or ate only squash. I exhausted myself teaching tennis, working eight to ten hours a day. If a spoonful or two of olive oil was good for me, I figured more must be better. And if meditating for fifteen or thirty minutes was a good idea, meditating all day long must be better. And, if living a spiritual life meant letting go of all attachments to material things, I gave away everything remotely valuable like a beautiful pearl evening purse that Sam had given me or an extraordinarily fine, pink, silk kimono that he had brought back from Japan for me. Everything material went.

I never told Gianni, I was too embarrassed, but my eating habits in the past, before squash, had been even more extreme. At one time I only ate the nuts out of fruitcakes. Period. On another jag, it was stewed apples and cheddar cheese only. Then there was the peanut butter and lettuce phase. Extremism, it seemed, had been my middle name. Had this been something created from my serious tennis days while being programmed to be a champion? It's hard to know. It was helpful to be aware of it.

As I looked back at my life, I could see the pattern. From tennis, tennis, tennis, I went to men, men, men, then dancing, dancing to teaching, teaching, to books, books and finally meditation. "Balance" was the answer. So "balance" became my mantra.

*

Life is everything. Guard it with everything you've got!

*

I had been reckless with my life. It was time to take care of it.

19 A GOAL OF BALANCE

A Balancing Act

I always seemed to have something that I was striving for. I needed a goal… another Wimbledon, I suppose. Balance was it. That's what I needed. I prayed for balance. I focused on balance. I wrote "balance" in my yellow sketchbooks over and over. I stared at the word, trying to absorb it into my being by osmosis.

At someone's suggestion, I read Florence Scovel Shinn's book *The Power of the Spoken Word* and learned about thoughts and their effects. I began watching my speech to make sure that I was not putting something into the ethers that I did not wish to see manifest, or rather only stating something that I wanted. "I am strong. I am healthy. I am balanced," I would say again and again.

On one of Michael's rare visits to the Boni's home, I noticed that he seemed to have a cold and I mentioned it. "No," he said. "I'm perfect." Obviously, he knew the power of words and would state only the positive. In this way he was supporting and encouraging his cells; he knew they were aware. How little we recognize the damage wrong thoughts and words can do and the value of being positive.

Michael shared with us his mantra, given to him by Ramana: "I am divine, nothing but divine, and my form is existence, consciousness and bliss. I am eternally free for that is my nature." For me he included the line, "without any sorrow," after the word "bliss." He must have known that I carried some "sorrow" from my family's lineage as well as from my own history. I use the mantra to this day. Its powerful message has a warming feeling. The truth usually does.

Life went on at the Boni's, and I proceeded to gain strength and understanding. Gatherings continued in the evenings, not only with the Geminis, but also with other interesting people. One of these was with the amazing Kathryn Walsh, a celebrated psychic and a good friend of Therese. She was a wildly flamboyant woman with fluffy, red hair that spilled out around her face in a way that drew attention away from her abundant figure, often covered in flouncy, floral dresses. On one particular evening she took center stage after dinner and started answering questions. In my turn with Kathryn, I asked about my future. She told me that I would marry and have a child. I was skeptical. Without a period, how was this possible? (This condition is typical of anorexic females, although Gianni never used the word "anorexic," yet that was certainly what I was.) Perhaps she meant that I would marry someone who had a child or children. This was not too far-fetched considering my history. "No," she said. "You will bear a child." I gave it no further thought.

Returning to My Life

Eventually, I was strong enough to live on my own again, so I returned to my apartment. I had some work to do…

cleaning it physically with buckets of soapy water and a mop, and psychically by spreading white light all over the place. I had transgressed royally and had gotten thumped. This was what I could do to make amends and clean the atmosphere.

I got back to work, mostly on my little children's books. My apartment was spotless on every level. I was full of joy from the care that I had received and the awareness I had gained, and eternally grateful for the kindness bestowed on me by so many.

It was an autumn afternoon when my brother called; our mother had died. It made me smile to think of her… her warmth and generosity were permanently with me. I was quite immune to feelings of sadness about this news. It was just the way it was; no wishing it were different. Ever since I had heard the story of Toddi's passing, I viewed death in a different way. So, I decided to honor my mother and help her by sending love and light to her off and on for the next few days. I would just think of her and let my love pour out to her. She must have felt it because I did.

A few days later, I met my brother at Leisure World in Laguna at my mother's condo. It was a lovely setting, something she created herself. The colors were hers… soft, velvety light blue for the couch with armed chairs to complement it in salmon pink. A large oil painting that I had done while I was at Oxy hung on the wall. It was of the eucalyptus trees that surrounded the campus. I had added a bit of an orangey pink to the leaves to make the painting match her décor. It was fun to please her. She so valued and encouraged my art through the years.

My brother Bob had let my mother's friends know that we would be there if they should want to stop by for a visit. One of her sweet friends came in and sat in a chair near the window. As she spoke, there was a large, blue light that followed her words. "We are all together in love," she said. The light made a swish, like the Nike swoosh, in the air behind her, almost as if it were an exclamation point. It was a special moment. Yes, this was true. My mother had gone nowhere. She had never left my love for her. That's where she'll always be.

My reaction to my mother's passing was much different from that of my reaction to my father's two years earlier. I had no understanding of these things at the time. My heart was broken when he died and I suffered terribly from this loss for quite awhile. (It is amazing how a different thought, a different point of view, can elicit a different reaction.)

My teaching resumed. My writing continued. I rode my bike, and with my friend television game show creator Chuck Barris, I played some paddleball. We played in a tournament together at the beach and surprised everyone by winning it. He sent me a note with our city ranking of number ten circled and the words, "How do you like them apples?"

During this time, I was focusing heavily on the heart-center and all my writings were about the heart and love. Of course, as The Law of Affinity would have it, Chuck sent me a lovely hanging plant for my apartment in which all the leaves were in the shape of hearts.

Chuck was a Gemini too and like all Geminis, we enjoyed each other's company. He gave me a beautiful, hunky, silver Mark Cross pen. Chuck was always doing things like that. If you said, you liked something, he would just give it to you. I used it to write and sketch stories in my Zora's sketchbooks. Then, one day the pen stopped working. Oh my, I took it to Mark Cross in Beverly Hills for repair. They lost it. Oh my, however they did replace it with a new one. It was not the same. I was quite sure that I wouldn't be able to write another story. I failed to realize that I was the one holding the pen. But then I got to wonder: who is holding me? Where do these stories come from?

A New Possibility

I checked in with the Bonis now and then. Gianni threw a thought out to me. "Why don't you take a session with Dr. Martha Frank?" I had met her once at the Bonis' and knew she was a distinguished child physiologist. Why not? What for I did not know.

Entering Dr. Frank's office in Pacific Palisades was like returning to my childhood. Small low tables were scattered around the room with little chairs to go with them and all sorts of toys, games, paper and paint, musical instruments, and balls. Everything I loved. The room had a low ceiling, fitting for the petite Dr. Frank. It was filled with light coming in from a wall of windows that looked out onto a serene Japanese garden. It was an older building and cozy, just like Dr. Frank.

I brought my box of children's books to show her. She studied them, and then gave me a few suggestions. "You have to be concrete with children when writing, rather than conceptual." Yes, these little books were too esoteric. "The images need to be complete with connected lines and not vague images." This was going to be hard for me as my line work and solid areas of color worked in tandem. I'd have to think about this.

She asked me a few questions about my life. I told her that I loved to dance. "Wonderful," she said. "Dance for me." I did not need to be asked twice. I floated through the air, spinning and twirling, my feet moving to some mystical music in my head.

When I stopped, she said, "You have such joy, where is the man in your life?" What man? I had forgotten about men and had been living a monastic life since I ventured on a spiritual path. A man? I wondered to myself. I hadn't thought about having a man in my life for quite some time. I was in love with life now and it seemed quite enough.

When I left Dr. Frank's playroom, I started thinking about this. Why not have a man in my life? By the time I reached my apartment, I knew how I would do it.

Previously, men had picked me and I had gone along with it. But this would be different; I would do the picking. So, I set about to create my man. I had a plan and I knew it would work. I would make it happen!

*

Love is all there is worth having or giving or being.

*

Yes, why not expand my heart and my world of love?

20 A PLAN FOR MY MAN

Creating my Man

Knowing that the Sun was the perfect representative of the divine in our realm, I decided to enlist his help. From my spiritual experiences, I knew that everything was alive and conscious; therefore, I wanted to seek help from the most miraculous and powerful being I could. The Sun was my choice. Therefore, I wrote a letter to the Sun and I wrote it in the present tense because I knew that my man already existed. I knew that if I were looking for him, he was looking for me. Here was my letter:

Dear Sun, please send me my man (I was tired of having someone else's man.) ***Here are the qualities of my man:*** (I wanted to make sure that I got exactly what I wanted.)

He is loving. To me, being a loving person was the most important quality on my list. I had discovered that love was the most important thing in my life, so I definitely wanted him to be loving.

He is kind. Just like loving, kindness was necessary. He must be a kind man who appreciated others and cared about their situations, their struggles. This was important to me.

He is good. I wanted a really good man; good to the core, a person whose intentions were always the best. My previous experiences around high-powered men led me to believe that their intentions were not always good. I guess I expected him to be high-powered.

He is intelligent. Oh, yes, I wanted an intelligent man who was clear-thinking, made good decisions, and had a curious mind. He must be open-minded, loved learning and valued intellectual challenges.

He is generous. My man, the one I was dreaming up, easily shared himself and what he had with others, and was delighted to do so.

He is happy. Equal on my list to being loving was being happy. I wanted a happy, optimistic man, one who knew his own worth and relished it.

He is athletic. It would be wonderful if he were athletic, even better if he played tennis. I knew our life together would take us to exciting and beautiful places and that would be better if we enjoyed each other in activities we loved… like tennis.

He wants a family. He loved children and appreciated family life. (Perhaps Kathryn was right. Maybe there was room in my life for my own child. Gianni had healed my body enough to make this possible.)

He is responsible. Responsibility was a sub-category of good in my book.

He is handsome. Why not? No one else had to think he was handsome, but I wanted a man who was handsome to me… a healthy, solid, wholesome, good-looking man.

He is faithful. In my heart of hearts, I was monogamous and I wanted my man to be the same. I understood the wandering hearts of some men, yet romance would remain in our marriage, I was sure of it, even if it were only holding hands on a long walk in our old age.

Yep, marriage was what I was asking for now… a down to earth, full-fledged, stick-together-through-thick-or-thin, for better or worse MARRIAGE!

This was what I wrote on one of the pages in my yellow sketchbook, then I tore it out and taped it on a window where the Sun could see it and no one else could.

Getting Ready

I knew that it was not enough to put in an order to the Universe, through the Sun, especially one like this. I needed to do some work. I needed to make an effort to show my sincerity of intent. First, I needed to spiff up my living accommodations. As a minimalist, my apartment was pretty sparse. Perhaps a charming, whicker rocking chair would be fun. This I found at a local second-hand store, brought it home and painted it. I set it on the west side of my living room, across from my art tables where I worked every day. He'd want to know where I worked. I tried the chair out and imagined him rocking in it. It was perfect! The arms were broad to hold his arms. To go with the rocker, a tea set was purchased from Pier One. They had interesting products from China that looked pricier than they were. Surely, he would like a spot of tea. New sheets, of course, and several flowering potted plants were added. I made my little abode as cozy as I could.

Then, I needed to get myself ready. I looked in the mirror and sized myself up. I was a little skinny by anyone's account. A few pounds needed to be added, so I prepared to bulk up. Because I was teaching tennis and playing a good bit of social tennis, I remained trim, but trim with some curves would be better. I ate more.

Next, I got an appointment with Hollywood's darling for hair design at the time, Peter York, who styled my hair into a lovely, soft pageboy. A little trim for $200 seemed appropriate for such an auspicious occasion, the meeting with my man. I left looking very glam and feeling like a poodle that had just been styled.

Peter York's haircut

My dear mother, who had seen me careen off of several walls in my life, not necessarily understanding my actions, but always loving me regardless, left me a little money in her will. This I used for a bit of shopping. My favorite haunt was Country Club Fashions in Beverly Hills. Everything in this shop was trendy and tasty. When I walked in the door, the saleslady asked me what I was looking for. "A dress," I said. She wanted to know for what occasion. "My wedding," I answered.

With much fluttering about, she helped me pick out a beautiful teal green silk crepe number. It went perfectly with some shoes I already had and it would look especially stunning with my Japanese happy coat. Happy was my present state; I knew he was on the way.

Now came the most important part of the scheme. I had to live as if it had already happened. This required that I be in love before I ever met the man I would be in love with. My routine was to think about this letter on my window and all that it contained every night before I fell asleep and send love to my man from my heart. It was as if he were on a trip and would be coming home soon. I sent love to him and thought about our life together… what we would do, where we would go. I remained ecstatically happy, living within this scenario that I had created.

Next, I followed any intuitive feeling I had that would send me in a direction, and I accepted all invitations to gatherings and events. I didn't know where or when he would show up. I just knew he would.

This again was that wonderful state of being on the way to something breath-taking that was almost better than arriving. The anticipation, the possibilities, the unexpectedness were all on the path, yet the outcome was certain because I had it down on paper and in my heart.

The Power of Love

Being in love, as I was at this point, created some unusual and awkward situations. Suitors were coming out of the woodwork. Love is the greatest of all attractors. It attracts like nothing else. As many friends as I told, "You must be in love before you find the one to be in love with" ... no one believed me. Most people are so linear. Being slightly dyslexic, time and space whirl a bit for me, so it was easy for me to take things out of sequence. I could easily "leave my rational mind behind." Yes, therein lay the secret to connecting with that special one: love him first and you'll draw him to you. That's what I believed. And, if what Michael preached were true, "As you think, so it will be," I was right on target.

In the meantime, before I connected with mister right, several mister wrongs came into my life. How could they not; I was splashing joy and effervescence wherever I went. I was in love!

The first of these was a Czechoslovakian artist friend of Milos Forman. He was brought to Jennings Lang's home by Milos to show his work. Jennings was a great collector of art and a soft touch to help a visiting artist such as Vasili. Vasili was an impressive man, dark, strong, with romantic, penetrating eyes that he directed at me.

After a tennis lesson with Milos, and along with Jennings, the four of us sat together in the tennis house near the pool. With Brancusis and Henry Moores dancing among the rose bushes in the garden, Vasili's art lay heavy and somber on the table, but his attention rested on me. And while

Milos promoted his friend's art to Jennings, the friend promoted himself to me.

We went to lunch. We went for tea. We went for dinner. He vowed his love and was sure I was the one for him. As many good qualities as he had, I was not sure that until-death-do-us-part was the right picture with this man. When I got back to my apartment, I looked at the letter I had written to the Sun and tried to match this man with my list of requirements. They didn't match.

Candidate Number Two

On I went. Following my plan to accept all invitations, I was invited to play tennis in an international tournament in a small town outside of Lagos, Nigeria. All expenses would be paid, so I packed up my bags, rackets and heart, and off I went.

Man number two showed up on a dance floor.

It happened like this. Because the heat was so unbearable in this venue, all the players in the tournament practiced in the mornings, rested during the day before playing their matches in the evenings. After which, the players danced the rest of the night. At least I did.

It was under the twinkling lights on a patio dance floor that I met Richard, suitor number two. He was a successful English entrepreneur who had a lucrative lumber business in the area. He was charming, entertaining, thoughtful, intelligent, handsome, rich – and a good dancer. I liked his European flair, his ruddy good looks, and the way he made me feel – like a princess. He was quite sure I was the one for him and fell in love with me almost upon meeting.

It was what I was sending out, I later realized, that drew these suitors to me. But as attractive as Richard was, and as many fine qualities as he possessed, I never imagined in all my imaginings that I would be living with my man in a place so remote and unbearably hot as Nigeria. In his kindness he nursed me through a bad case of the "flu," saw me safely on my plane back to the U.S. and accepted my rejection of his proposal of marriage with graciousness.

When I returned to California, I discovered that the "flu" was not exactly the "flu," but rather an obscure strain of malaria.

It made itself known when at a Thanksgiving dinner party with my brother, his family, and his in-laws, I had to excuse myself from the table to go put on my coat, a new coat. They all thought I wanted to show it off; instead, I was freezing. After checking my temperature, my brother drove me to UCLA Medical Center; the local hospital would not take me. It was nothing they could deal with. Tests upon tests were given to me at UCLA. Doctors and students filled my hospital room.

"Didn't you take your anti-malaria pills when you were in Africa?" the doctors asked.

"What anti-malaria pills?" I asked. Yes, I had made the arrangements in haste and had probably not read the details of what I needed to do to prevent something like this.

Fever does odd things to you. I was fairly odd to begin with, now this situation compounded it. In my feverish delirium I insisted that all I needed was just some diluted fruit juice and rest. "Just leave me be. I'll be fine." That was my remedy for everything. I never went to doctors. No. With my temperature hitting 107 degrees, I would not be fine. More unbalance ensued. I was quite sure that the medication they were giving me was causing my temperature to rise. It was not until I spoke with Dr. Boni by phone that I trusted the UCLA medical staff and followed their procedures. That consisted of three days of medication at exact intervals and I would truly be fine. And so, I was... a little thinner and a lot weaker.

A period of recuperation followed and I returned to my happy plan of meditating, creating books, playing and teaching tennis and dreaming of my Sun Man. In the books I wrote and illustrated, several interesting characters began to appear – a beautiful woman with lovely soft under-turned hair, a handsome man and a little boy. In one story the little boy had a pet rabbit. Was this a precursor to reality?

*

Picture a happy life

and soon you will be able to put a frame around it.

*

The Law of Affinity was definitely at work as always.

21 THE REAL DEAL

Out of the Blue

Besides teaching on Jennings' court, I was occasionally invited to play social tennis there on weekends with a group of his friends. And again, true to my vow of saying "yes" to all invitations, when Jennings' secretary called, I agreed to play in a group one Saturday morning in October. She added, "Bring along some of your artwork. A man from Hallmark is going to be there!"

"Of course. Of course." Jennings was always trying to help my art career and even thought I could do a panel for newspapers, combining my thoughts with my illustrations. Little did he know that many years later, this idea would come into being. But at this point, he thought Hallmark might be a perfect fit for me.

So, on the day I was to meet the man from Hallmark, I put on my prettiest Teddy Tinling tennis dress, dabbed on my favorite perfume, Fracas, gathered up my artwork and tennis rackets and headed for Jennings' home.

As I walked through the sculpture garden meandering down toward the court, there was the sweet smell of something special in the air. Was it just autumn, or was it something else?

This court was one of my favorite courts that I had ever played on. Situated in a ravine, and surrounded on three sides by eucalyptus trees, it needed no tarps. The trees provided the backdrop and the birds living in them provided the music.

I took a seat at one of the tables on the covered patio over-looking the court. The playful sounds of the players joking with each other drifted up.

I sat patiently waiting my turn to play while the others finished their set.

I was called onto the court to be Jennings' partner. Across the net was Alan Berman, the Academy Award winning songwriter, and Marv Huss, the man from Hallmark. While Marv reached for my hand in greeting, his smile overwhelmed me with warmth. He was delicious, an oatmeal cookie, an All-American type, wholesome and handsome at the same time, and a bit old-fashioned like his name. There was a force about him that made me know I should pay attention to this man, and not just for my artwork. There was also that blue light again. It filled the sky behind him. I had seen that light once before but at that time it was just a small light. This time it was huge. It was a sign!

I had a hard time focusing on the ball as we played. I passed him at net a few times. He laughed. He put away my lobs. I laughed. He was someone I knew, but was just meeting for the first time.

After that set, we sat courtside and he rummaged through my portfolio, with him making complimentary and encouraging remarks. The truth was that he found my art too esoteric for Hallmark, although he said he liked them. I'm not sure he really liked them; he may have liked the concepts. It didn't really matter to me; I liked him. Once we were done with that, I didn't want our time together to end, so I asked if he had played enough tennis for the day. "No," he said.

"Well, I'm going out to Malibu to play some more," I said. "Would you like to go along?"

"Yes," he answered.

We motored out to The Malibu Colony in my snappy MGBGT. We cruised down the lane between the homes until we came upon some of my tennis buddies: Bob MacLeod, in his 60's and still editor of Teen Magazine; Albie Linnick, a rogue attorney; Dick Greenberg, a real estate mogul; and the actors Jack Warden and Robert Duvall. We were welcomed in and played a set or two, and then we slipped through Bob's house to the beach.

The sun was still high, although closing down the day. The waves threw some mist our way, and the beach, which was never very crowded, was empty except for us… or so it seemed. All I saw was this beautiful man.

It was there, I think, that I fell in love with this man from Hallmark. As we walked along, he told me about his life, his work as head of advertising for Hallmark, his admiration for its founder, Joyce Hall, whom he worked for directly, and his efforts in providing the best possible programs for the Hallmark Hall of Fame television series. That was why he was in town, to purchase the rights to "The Snow Goose" from Jennings at Universal Studios for Hallmark's television series.

In all this small talk, he revealed himself. I knew the core of this man was good. His intentions were good and his gestures generous. He matched my enthusiasm for life. He was heartfelt and I was heart-struck.

That wasn't the end of it, our conversation continued over dinner and dancing that evening. It was a perfect day.

Before I put my head on my pillow that night, I took my Sun Letter off the window and read it again. He was everything on my list – Marv was the one. There was no question about it from my point of view, besides there'd been a blue light. He was my dream come true. He was my Sun Man, even though he let me know that he was married and had three kids. Not surprising, this had been my modus operandi.

A Waiting Period

It took two more years before we finally got together. There were a few obstacles to be cleared away. He lived across the country from me and had a very exciting career with responsibilities that had to be attended to.

So, during that time, Marv sent me cards from Hallmark

and I sent him card designs for Hallmark. I sent him a pair of sunglasses that he said he was forever losing. He sent me more cards from Hallmark. Our favorite song by Stevie Wonder included the words, "You are the sunshine of my life. You're the apple of my eye." So, I sent him a crystal apple for his desk. He sent me still more cards from Hallmark. Then he left Hallmark and moved from Kansas City to Denver to start his own advertising agency.

Marv, the apple of my eye

To pass the time while waiting for Marv's life to rearrange itself, two things occurred. The first was that I was in a horrible automobile accident. I was on my way to visit my brother and his family in Orange County and I stopped at a wide intersection in the left lane, the fast lane. When the light turned green, I accelerated straight into the side of a produce truck whose driver had decided to turn left in front of me, against his red light. Everything was totaled... my car, the bike on the back of it, the produce truck, fortunately not the other driver or me. I knew immediately the message: I had to be stopped. I was driving too fast. I was moving too fast in life. Yes, the happier I was, the faster I moved. This made me a danger to others. Even though this "accident" was not my fault. It was truly my fault for flying too high, too wildly, too recklessly. Harmony was the answer. Would I ever reach it?

As I had gone into the windshield during the crash, my face was rearranged, almost unrecognizably so, with black eyes and a hematoma on my forehead so large that it had to be drained each day. I was a mess.

Wobbling from this near disaster, I struggled again for balance, gauging my steps and my energies. It was a fine line, this state of balance.

I remember Therese many times recalling Hermes Trismegistus' caution regarding life… that it should be traversed as if one were on a tightrope walking across a deep crevasse… very carefully.

I gathered myself together and slowly worked back into a sensible routine… tennis and writing books, and also loving my Sun Man from a distance.

Back on Tour

The second event that occurred during this waiting period was a return to a somewhat competitive environment. I had never played on the Pacific Northwest tennis tour; I'd always been sent off to play internationally. With the money my mother left me, I joined a friend with whom I could play doubles and off we went. It was the first time I could test my new approach to tennis… the relaxed, fearless, formless, full-of-it, carefree style that I had been teaching… in an actual competitive tournament. The results (although the results were not my focus) were outstanding. I won the championships in Tacoma, Seattle, and Vancouver and was moved onto the pro satellite circuit. There I won an important match or two, which filtered me into the draws on the major tour, the Virginia Slims Tennis Circuit. I was playing in a competitive setting without competing. In other words, I didn't go after the other player; I went after the ball. I was fearless. I could not be beaten. The other player might win the match, but I could not be beaten! This attitude annoyed many players; none wanted to play me. If I didn't care if I won or lost, I was free... and free to be very powerful and free to win.

This circuit was the precursor to what is now the Women's Pro Tour. In fact, at that point money had been introduced to the game, although I gave it no consideration. I was just out for a lark and if I won a match or two... fine. I was enjoying the scenery in the area where a tournament was being played and spent no time with the other players or training. My training was to go out every night and dance. I could walk into a nightclub, pick up a partner, dance my socks off, and disappear before I could get into any trouble, or trouble could get to me. It was as if I were protected in some way because I went into some very dingy clubs. It was all about the movement. I think the boldness and assertiveness with which I moved kept me safe.

It was interesting to see the difference that money had made to the game, more precisely to competitive tennis. Keep in mind; my serious tennis was played before money, now I was playing where money was at stake. This brought a completely different element into the game. No longer was this a game for the elite; it was a game for athletes. They smelled the money and started hitting tennis balls. These players also showed up on the tour with pushy parents and coaches and counselors of all kinds. Calls were disputed, umpires were disrespected, linesmen were admonished, and ball children were never thanked. This was cutthroat tennis with much of the grace cut out of the game. I was shocked and kept my distance. Many times, the tournament director would say to me, "I have a check for you from the last tournament." It was something I wasn't used to, but I didn't let it get in my way of having fun – whether I won or lost a match.

When the tour passed through Denver, Marv and I met again. My particular tournament match was farmed out to Colorado Springs. I ended up having a big win for me at the time, knocking off the world's number four-ranked player. Sitting in the stands on center court after the match, Marv and I mapped out our future together. His career had changed and he was ready to change everything.

He had had enough of corporate life and wearing suits and ties. We decided to teach tennis together and perhaps run a club together, if we could find one.

When I finished the tour, I returned to California, packed my bags and wicker rocker and moved to Colorado Springs to be closer to Marv. And he in turn began restructuring his life to be with me. There were children involved, older now, but still he needed to help them find their way.

My little cottage in Colorado Springs was perfect for my life now. I taught a bit of tennis, went back to writing stories, and rendezvoused with Marv in Denver as often as possible. On one of these occasions, while I was still a bit flighty, he visited me at the Holiday Inn for breakfast, mumbled something, and planned to return at the end of the day. When he did arrive later, he announced, "You must be the happiest girl in the world!" I was not sure exactly why, but I played along.

"I am. I am," I said with a big smile, still puzzled.

"Because I've asked you to marry me!" (I just loved a confident man!)

"Of course. Of course," I said, covering my oversight. What a thing to miss!

During my time in Colorado Springs, I made contact with a man who wanted to build a resort in Aspen. He needed a manager to oversee the construction and manage the project. And he needed a head rackets pro. We filled both bills.

*

Everyday occurrences might just be ordinary miracles.

*

It took patience to let things work out the way I hoped they would. Patience is always a challenge. Letting go seems to be the answer.

22 A REAL MARRIAGE

Aspen Delight

Marv and I married on a beautiful Halloween morning in Aspen in 1976. I wore my teal green dress. Marv's parents flew in on a tiny plane that nearly scared my future mother-in-law to death. Tiny planes were the only way to fly into Aspen. My brother's family didn't mind and their children added their sparkle to the celebration. One was a ring bearer, another a flower girl, and the youngest carried a pumpkin.

Wedding day with brother Bob and family in Aspen

We spent three glorious years there building The Aspen Club and filling it with members. Marv was a promotional genius and created unusual activities to build the membership for this new club, which had to worm its way into a town of 3,000 that already had five other tennis clubs.

For one of the promotional events, Marv brought in the Grand Champions

Marv in his flight suit in earlier days

I didn't realize what I had in this Sun Man. I had had little experience with military men... and this was a Marine! He had not only been a Marine, but a fighter pilot who had flown on and off carrier ships in the Pacific. His confidence level was extraordinary; there was nothing that he couldn't do.

He had come from a very modest home with caring, but uneducated parents. To dare to go to UC Berkeley and defy his father, a union leader who had landed him a job in a Swift meat packing operation, took a strong will. Baseball and basketball coaches recruited him to Cal. Then, once he got his teeth into education, sports took a back seat like the meat packing company.

After graduation, he joined the Marines. When he saw planes flying overhead, he asked an officer how he could do that. He had never been in an airplane. By the time his stint was up, he had qualified in single engine props, single engine jets, twin-engine props and helicopters.

How did he do it? Very simply, he had the courage to try anything that was productive. He made the effort. That was the same drive that landed him at Hallmark and in charge of the Hallmark Hall of Fame.

So, building and promoting a tennis and health club in Aspen was a piece of cake for him.

A Small Battle of the Sexes

One of these promotions Marv that created pitted me against the ultimate chauvinist pig, Bobby Riggs. It was soon after his world-famous loss to Billie Jean King and soon after my coming off of the women's tour. I was in fine fiddle, but was he? It was a festive affair with Bobby arriving with his "nurse" and asking to be taken immediately to the nearest doctor for a cortisone shot for his elbow. He wore a tight "Sugar Daddy" t-shirt, which was obviously two sizes too small and designed to prove that he was definitely out of shape and easy pickings for those who wanted to bet against him. This was classic Riggs, who was notorious for arriving at any club in the country and ripping off the membership, one by one, in antics from playing tennis with an ashtray instead of a racket, or playing with a chair tied to his leg.

Aspen welcomed him for the three-day event. Each citizen, and others who had flown in or driven in from out of town, took their turn betting against him on something... like which fly would leave the wall first, or who would walk in the door next, a man or woman? There were games of backgammon, golf, and unusual pairings of tennis teams that challenged him.

Our attorney, Andy Hecht, held the money for the major competition, our match. The town was humming with excitement. Everyone wanted to get in on the action. Everyone was quite sure that I would beat this old codger; after all, I had beaten every male pro in town. However, I had seen Bobby up to his antics at the L.A. Tennis Club long before and I was not convinced. Unfortunately, Marv let me know the night before the match that he had bet $1,000 on me, a tidy sum in my thinking and also my thinking didn't include gambling. Pressure-free tennis was my preferred manner of play. Now I had the whole town, plus my husband's investment on my back for this match.

That night I had a dream that I lost a million dollars. The message was clear, but the bet was set. All I could do was play out the match as graciously as I could, while being beaten as handily as Bobby was capable of doing. The entertainment value was outstanding with Bobby hitting trick shots that would cross the net, reverse themselves and return to his side without my even touching them. He served inside out shots and hit drop shots, and managed to run down everything I sent his way.

Sly fox Bobby Riggs during our match

Our attorney Andy had been the sparring partner for Bobby each day prior to the big match and would report to Marv. "He can hardly hit the ball in the court. Sally won't have a problem," he said. However, on his warm up before the big match, Andy reported, "He's a different player!" I knew it. I'd had the dream.

Bobby was hardly off the court after our match before he was swished away to the golf course at Snowmass for a round of golf before his plane took off, and to collect some more loot from some more suckers. These blokes were delighted to have a go at him and ultimately give him their bucks for the stories they would be able to tell their grandchildren.

It was a great weekend and as Marv stuffed Bobby's pockets with all his winnings and the original $5,000 prize money, Bobby, with Nurse Nancy in tow, climbed the stairs of the plane. "Any time, Marv," he called back. "I loved it!" So did we and we filled the club with members in the process.

More Fun Events

Marv continued to come up with fun events for club members or visitors to the club. There was the "Tea and Trumpets Round-Robin" mixed doubles tournament that used every court in town and every player.

Virtuoso violinist Itzak Perlman plays with the perpetual trophy

It was to benefit the Aspen Music Festival there. The locals loved the music festival. You could walk around the village and hear young musician practicing their art, and preparing for their seminars with the greatest musicians in the world. It was the highlight of every summer. On the final day of the tournament, the money from the entry fees, which was substantial, was handed over to Itzak Perlman, representing the music festival. He, in turn, handed over the winners' trophy to Marv and me.

Another guest, Rod Laver stopped in for a visit one weekend. He and his wife Mary had come to Aspen on holiday. Mary liked to ski; Rod did not. So, we created a little round robin for him to keep him occupied as well as entertain the members.

Attorney Andy Hecht and Rod after some social doubles

More celebrities stopped by the club. World Heavy Weight Boxing Champion Ingemar Johansson was found on the volleyball court hitting a punching bag and disturbing the local interclub basketball game. Marv was called upon to remove him. The locals were more interested in their activities than Ingemar's.

Arnold Schwarzenegger, before his fame, tried to talk Marv into some kind of exhibition of his physical prowess. Nope. The members liked to do their own thing.

Then there was Clint Eastwood, an old friend from California. For him we created an impromptu tournament and gave him Linda McCausland, a local mover-shaker, for a partner. We thought it would tickle her fancy. It seemed to.

Partners Linda and Clint

And Baby Makes Three

During our time in Aspen, I became pregnant, just as Kathryn Walsh so long ago had predicted. Then, Merv Griffin made good on his promise to see my tennis book, *How to Play Power Tennis with Ease*, get into publication. My editor panicked at my naivety when I let her know that I was about to give birth and would do all of the illustrations for the book after the baby was born. "I'll have plenty of time," I said.

"Can't you do it before?" she asked, after her office had a good laugh. I had no idea how much work a baby could be. I was thirty-eight and all of my contemporaries had kids in high school and couldn't remember what the baby phase was like. They were no help. Marv was no help in this area either, as he was in the service and not home when his first three sons were born.

"Of course, I can do the illustrations before the baby arrives," I told my editor.

Baby Michael arrives

The book came and went. Now, with many additions and alterations I have rewritten it, summarizing what I had learned in my many years of teaching and playing. Presently, it is titled *Eight Golden Rules for How to Play Your Best*

Tennis. It garnered glowing reviews from Mary Carrillo, Dick Enberg, Billie Jean King, and others. Billie was always supportive of my books. We were junior players at the same time, although I was a couple of years older.

With Billie Jean at the National 40's Championships in Chicago

Aspen was lovely in the seventies – not as glitzy as it is today, of course, but glitzier than it had been. Besides this swank and glamor, the one thing that you couldn't miss was how much the locals loved to be there. They loved Aspen! They were outdoor people who loved to bike, hike, kayak, play soccer in the park, and ski. Aspen not only had the sparkle that money brought to the town, it had the most beautiful mountain wilderness you could imagine – Aspen Mountain, Snowmass, Buttermilk, Maroon Bells. It was like a fairyland when it snowed. It snowed often – big, fat, fluffy flakes that made skiers everywhere wish they were there. That beauty attracted the rich and famous and, unfortunately it gained notoriety for some of the era's hedonistic excesses. The mayor finally cracked down and declared that there would be no more open use of cocaine in the restaurants.

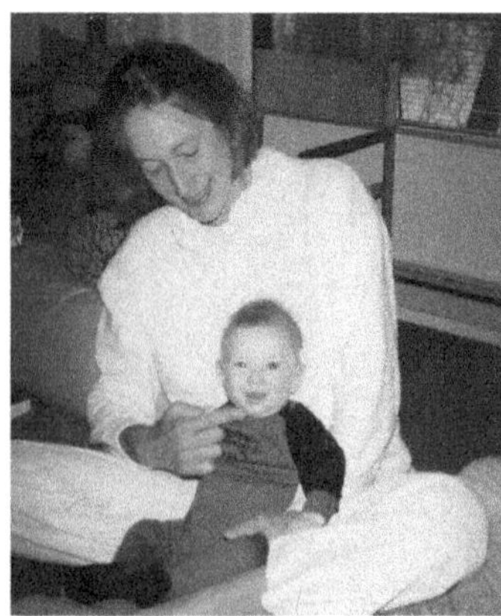

Michael and his adoring parents

John Denver wrote his songs there. Olympic skier Spider Sabich was shot and killed by a jealous lover there. And we built a lovely tennis/health club there.

Proud father, bewildered son

Our life together was full of extraordinary experiences and enriched by outstanding people we met along the way.

All of this life with Marv was foretold in pictures and words in my sketchbooks, brought about through the Law of Affinity, also known as the Law of Correspondence or Attraction, by my Sun Letter, my imagination and my love for what I wanted!

Changes of Venues

Now our wants were different. With baby Michael in the picture, we wanted to be out of the fast lane. As it happened, we owned part of a tennis dress line and decided to move with it to North Carolina, home of the fabric industry, and to a sleepy little town called Greenville. We arrived with a hunk of money from the sale of our home in Aspen and tried to find something comparable in Greenville.

The real estate agent was stumped until she drove us to an exclusive area called Holly Hills that was filled with flowering azaleas, ponds, and magnificent magnolia trees. It was hidden from the hustle and bustle of the rest of the town. "How about that one over there," I said, pointing to a rambling, ranch style estate on several acres with two ponds of its own.

"I'll see if the owners will sell," she said.

Of course, they would. It was a California style oasis in the middle of all the other homes, each devoted to the North Carolina traditional Williamsburg style. The owners of this home had no children and had spent their years gardening and developing this extraordinary property. We were the beneficiaries.

I dabbled in a bit of art and ended up creating cartoons for World Tennis magazine, even publishing a small book of these tennis cartoons. As I look at the linework in these cartoons today, it looks mighty rough. Still the ideas were fun.

A sample of the cartoons that ran in World Tennis Magazine

Our son, Michael grew happily in this lovely environment, Marv did business, and I wrote, filling up my box of books. After a couple of years, we sold out of the dress company and were free to move again. California called this time.

Michael tickled with himself and taking after mom

*

Along every path beautiful experiences are gathered.

*

We had many beautiful experiences in Aspen and North Carolina, but more were waiting in California.

23 RETURNING TO CALIFORNIA

Familiar Territory

It was to the beach area that we headed. We settled in Newport Beach while Marv worked on a luxurious condominium project in Laguna Beach. He was gathering funds by the fistfuls, which we decided to use to create another tennis club like The Aspen Club, but this time it would be ours.

It was to be on a magnificent hilltop in Bonsall, north of San Diego. The twenty-two-acre site would be a destination resort, much in the style of John Gardiner's Tennis Ranch in Carmel Valley... classy, exclusive, elegant, and fun. Two of the problems with this plan were that Marv, as charming as he was, hardly knew how to mix a drink and my idea of being a hostess was to tell someone to go in the kitchen and fix whatever they wanted. I had no hostess skills or servant energy in me, and Marv didn't know one drink from the next. John Gardiner, our role model for this project, on the other hand, floated around his establishment, fulfilling every whim of his guests, whether it was food, drink, tennis, or swimming. He was just remarkable; the most gracious host I'd ever met.

Site of our future resort

The other drawback to this plan was that I kept trying to find a place on the property for my art studio. I wanted an art studio. My head was not really into tennis at this point and I was leaning into my art. Tons of money was spent on all the things we needed to create this project – architectural plans, surveys upon surveys, historical evaluations of the land, and endless requirements from the County, all of which increased the costs. They even insisted that we buy a new fire engine for the area.

Then just in the nick of time, I had a dream. We had been working for nine months to secure a loan to build this project. At last, the word came in that the loan was approved and the money was available. All we needed to do was drive to Palm Desert to sign the loan documents.

"Use your talents," the voice in the dream said, the night before we were to sign. I knew it didn't mean tennis… something else this time.

This probably would have been a deal breaker in most marriages. It was definitely a true test of ours when I announced at breakfast, "I'm not going to sign."

Marv sat dumbfounded, waited a moment, regrouped, and asked, "Then what are we going to do?"

"Art," I said. "Art!"

"Okay," he answered.

Dismantling a Dream

We returned the $10,000 that Kirk and Anne Douglas had given us to pre-book space in the future resort for some of their family members. They had been very supportive of our project and I would keep them updated on its progress during our visits with them in their Palm Springs home during the winter. It was always fun; their home was full of interesting people – singer Dinah Shore, actor Louie Jourdan, a few producers, some political types, and a handful of Lords and Ladies.

I found it amusing that Kirk would wander into the kitchen in the morning, looking like no one you had ever seen, and within an hour, life would flow back into his body and he would transform into Kirk Douglas again.

His wife Anne was the truly clever one. She ran the show without his ever knowing it. She dressed for the super market as if she were going to an awards banquet. She never knew who would be wandering around snapping photos. And she kept an eye on her man too. If he wandered out in front of their home in his red Speedo swimsuit to water some plants or something, she would rope him in. No gawking tourists in a tour bus were going to grab a shot of Kirk when he wasn't at his best! He, however, thought the Speedos showed him at his best; she did not.

We played tennis together on their court, and accompanied them to dinner parties at their friends' homes. One of those homes in particular was filled with priceless original Impressionist and Post-Impressionist art… Picassos, Braques, Degases, Manets, Cezannes, Monets, Gauguins, Cassatts, Sisleys, and the Douglases' favorites, the Van Goghs. My mouth dropped open as I wandered among the hallways where this collection hung.

Besides playing tennis with the Douglases, I would create amusing storyboards for them that they would hang here and there or give as gifts. I did a special one for their friend with all the masterpieces, Lord somebody. I was happy to know that my humble work of art was in good company, even if it were finally hung in the Lord's walk-in closet.

Along with returning the money to the Douglases, Marv had the task of unloading the property we had purchased for the project. This was not a problem for him; he was a natural when it came to real estate and had even dabbled in it when we were in Aspen. That's what kept us afloat... real estate.

Back to my Tennis Roots

Happiness had been a subject that I was studying... how it affected every facet of a person's life, where it came from, and how to maintain such a state. I loved writing about the subject – the more I did, the happier I got. This was certainly what I was emphasizing in the tennis teaching that I was doing. Then, it occurred to me that I could speak on this subject, especially in relation to tennis.

At the time, I had also returned to playing competitively in senior events. I played my happy-go-lucky style of tennis and let the results take care of themselves. They certainly did. My senior titles stacked up and national rankings followed (#1 national ranking in the Women's 40 Division, #1 national ranking in the Women's 45 Division, #1 in the 35, 40 and 45 Divisions in Southern California in the same year.)

A senior champion

Fred Perry visiting one of the senior events

But the curious thing was that I wasn't so much interested in the titles, as I was in the opportunity to book talks. As a "champion" I spoke to all kinds of groups, not just tennis or sports groups. There were the 5,000 nurses at their national convention. Michael, sitting in the audience with his father, said to Marv, "Mom's gonna die when she gets on stage and sees this!" There were other large and small gatherings… men's organizations, and youth groups. The talks were all about happiness… about getting happy, being happy, and staying happy. The theme had come to me at the end of a dream. The words I heard were: "If you wait to be happy, you will wait forever. If you are happy now, you will be happy forever." Wow! That's a thought that you could live with the rest of your life and it would enhance everything in it. It was a complete philosophy in itself.

Out of this focus on "happy talks," I created the most

Passing on a "Happy Philosophy" to a small group

amusing compilation of thirty exercises to bring a person greater joy. I called it *The Happy Book*. I printed it myself at Kinko's and made some adorable little disks out of kids' Play Dough to go with it. People loved it.

My entrepreneurial spirit kicked in and I thought if a few people liked it, so would a lot of people. I needed a publisher. Amazingly, that very year the National Book Expo was being held in Los Angeles. I packed up my sample book, put on my brightest and happiest Jams dress, and entered the L.A. Convention Center.

Aisles of books, booksellers, and publishers with their editors lined the hall. As life would have it, I ended up in the booth of Ten Speed Press, a hip publisher out of Berkeley. The main editor, Joann Deck, wandered over and said, "You have to meet Phil." Phil Wood was the owner of Ten Speed and only wore Jams clothes. He had over one hundred Jams' shirts with matching ties. He took my book in his hand, thumbed through it without looking at any page and said, "We'll publish it and you'll be happy with the deal." He "felt" the book and that was it. That was my second book published with a real publisher.

Later when that book was out of print, Ten Speed kindly returned the rights and I have self-published it under the title *The Importance of Living Happy*. No little disks go with it though.

More speaking engagements followed. Little Michael would accompany me on many of these adventures and sell books and small inspirational pieces of art in back of the room. Following my own preaching, I began spending more time on the art. It made me happy, in turn I made happy art!

Pretty happy about *The Happy Book*

Unusual Tennis

Along the way and still playing some pretty good tennis, I was included in several pro-am tournaments in and around L.A. and San Diego. Some of these put me in touch with old pros, and others with celebrities. Mike tagged along with me when his dad was working. He jumped right into the festivities.

Pro-am event in Irvine with Gene Wilder with matching hairdos

Even Ivan Lendle showed up at an event in Newport Beach

Still the best time Mike ever had on one of these junkets was the result of Marv reading an article in U.S.A. Today. It seemed that a Japanese company was introducing a new sport to the U.S. – soft tennis! It sounded fascinating. As usual, I was game for most anything, so he encouraged me to investigate. The Japanese company needed someone in the tennis community to connect them to tennis players and clubs in California. I was elected!

They sent me a boatload of equipment and a few instructions on how the game was played. It was a popular sport in Asia, especially Japan, Taiwan, South Korea, and India, but unknown in the States. It was played on a tennis court and was not too far off from tennis. However, the equipment was unfamiliar. The rackets were a size between a tennis and a badminton racket, and teardrop-shaped. But it was the ball that held the promise of something different. It was smaller than a tennis ball and made of thin rubber. It had to be pumped up to a particular size. Only doubles were played. Now when you hit this ball, and you could hit it as hard as you wanted, it never went out of the court. It was fun, just fun!

I did my job, connecting the Japanese to some topnotch tennis players and the game was off and running.

I bowed out of the promotion at one point and heard nothing more about it until a year later. A woman called me up and said, "I hear you play soft tennis. There's going to be a U.S. championship and if you win you get a free trip to Japan to play in the World Championships. Will you be my partner?"

I was in. We won the U.S. title, playing only one other team, and off to Japan we went, Mike and Marv too. We saw the sights of Tokyo, rode the bullet train, and landed in the sumo-wrestling stadium in Nagoya. Three matches were played contiguously. It was hectic with large crowds, each court's rooters yelling for their team at the same time.

It was the crowds that fascinated me – all dark-haired people who couldn't have been kinder. Amongst them were a large number of young girls, pre-teens… and they all seemed to love little tow-headed Michael. Every day they brought him gifts and took care of him while I played.

It was a different atmosphere than what we were used to. In the U.S. while we would hover over our child, especially in a crowd, it wasn't necessary there. Everyone was kind, helpful, and protective. He was safe.

With my partner receiving our award for "courage"

Well of course, my partner and I were no match for anyone who actually played this sport, but it was still fun. We did take a set off of the ultimate winners from South Korea. We only did this because they had never seen a slice. They were used to heavy topspin balls. Once they caught on to our slicing tactic, it was all over. At the end of the event, we were given an award for "courage."

Team Tennis

Through the years I have played on many teams, starting with the National Junior Wightman Cup Team.

Southern California Junior Wightman Cup Team at the Philadelphia Cricket Club with future Wimbledon Champion Karen Hantze on my left

Also, I was included on the real Wightman Cup Team, precursor to the Federation Cup. I played on two of those teams and played none too well.

National Junior Wightman Cup Team
on the sacred grounds of Forest Hills

Finally, I ended up playing on several national senior teams and competing in the U.S. and Europe.

U.S. 40's Team competing in France

Some of these events required travel. Sometimes Mike and Marv went with me, enjoying more than the tennis matches. One year it included a visit to the French Open. Such a treat!

Center Court at Roland Garros

Mike and mom in Paris after playing the ITF Senior 40's Cup

Lucky Winner

I continued to play senior events, sometimes playing two divisions in a tournament at the same time, i.e., the 35's and 45's, thus playing two semis on the same day and then two finals on the next. I don't know why I did it, other than to see if I could. Again, I was giving my little happy talks at the clubs where I played and getting happier by the minute. At one tournament in Huntington Beach during the end-of-tournament party I was presented two winners' trophies. Amazingly, someone drew my name out of a hat for the door prize – a clock. You'd think that was enough, until there was yet another drawing. This time it was for a family trip to Vancouver for the 1986 World's Fair. Yep, I won that too! Happiness really works.

Enjoying the puppet exhibit at the World's Fair

*

Kiss the day in the morning and surely it will

kiss you back by night.

*

Many changes sent us this way and that. Yet, following a happy path led us to our real destination.

24 THE GAME OF ART

Back to my Other Roots

With the help of our neighbor in Bonsall, where we now resided, I started building display easels and researching arts and craft shows. I studied them first to see what sold at these events and what were the best displays. In my research, I discovered an operation that was doing a gangbuster business. It sold small, framed pieces of art with verse. Nothing exceptional regarding the art and nothing original, I learned, regarding the words. They were just generic sayings. But the whole presentation was put together so well and attractively it was hard to walk by it without stopping. This became my model.

First outdoor art show, testing the product line

Michael was seven at the time and had been given a rabbit for Easter. We were just like the family I had envisioned years before in one of my little books. That box of books travelled with us wherever we moved. Since we were no longer in the resort-building mode, we up-rooted ourselves again and moved to San Clemente, California.

Dr. Boni with Michael

Michael went with me when I first ventured out into the world of business with easels and a tent at local arts and craft shows. We adorned our booth with colored banners and flags, colored wire baskets filled with inspirational gift art that would warm any heart. And with Marv's guidance from his Hallmark days, we created these pieces for anyone and everyone: mothers, daughters, fathers, brothers, grandparents, friends, and professionals. These were little works of art with original, happy sayings, all beautifully framed in the color of your choice. "Good enough for giving, as well as keeping," I would say. Originally, these pieces were hand-painted in acrylic. Eventually I moved on to having them printed.

We did shows up the Southern California coast – La Jolla, Laguna Beach, Costa Mesa, Huntington Beach, Redondo Beach, Santa Monica, and Malibu. On the first day of the Malibu show, we sold out of most all of the art. I returned home, painted all night, came back and sold everything again the next day.

At the Malibu show with niece Melissa and Larry Hagman, long before anyone knew who shot JR

My thrifty nature wouldn't allow me to throw away the leftover paint I was using for the gift art pieces; so I used it to paint a large canvas now and then. I had totally forgotten that I could paint or that I had a degree in fine art.

Our booth at art and craft shows

When the large paintings began to sell at shows, a design gallery in Laguna Beach wanted to sell them in their shop. Once they started selling there, Marv said, "Let's open our own gallery."

Marv's abilities as a marketer and businessman were the perfect complement to my artistic talents. Afterall, he had created the original Hallmark Card shops. Through this joint effort we were able to create a business that benefited many… not just the wonderful people who eventually worked for us, but those who collected one of these happy paintings, as well anyone who received one of the inspirational gift art pieces. There were also the people who would stop by our booth just to feed themselves by reading the messages in these small art pieces. It was like a whole philosophy wrapped up in these verses. If someone couldn't find a thought they wanted in the existing line, I would write one for them. It might be to help someone through a difficult time or to honor someone they loved. It was fun to do.

One of the first galleries

Our first gallery was on Coast Highway in Laguna Beach. The rent was $1,800 a month. I was terrified, not Marv. He was the courageous one. We put a large painting in the window while Marv was cleaning the floor preparing for our opening. The painting sold before Marv had finished the floor... for $1,800.

Marv came up with a great idea for the opening of the gallery. He was always coming up with great ideas for me to do. In this case, it was for me to paint a large 4′x6′ canvas we would give away in a drawing on a particular day. All anyone had to do was come into the gallery before that date and register for the drawing... but they had to be present at the drawing. Traffic stopped on Coast Highway on opening night. The gallery was overloaded. Police couldn't figure out what was going on. It was a huge success.

A very grand opening of Laguna Beach gallery

We used that same strategy for the openings of our other galleries. It was interesting to learn what people had done who won the drawings. They were people who focused intently on winning. One woman wanted the give-away painting so badly she had all of her family members sign up. She herself did not have the winning ticket, but her mother did who promptly gave her the painting. At another drawing, a young woman, who was very sick, insisted that her boyfriend bring her to the gallery. She knew she would win… and she did.

Center of the action on Santa Monica's Third Street Promenade

One Sally Huss Gallery became five in a short time, all were in Southern California, strung along the coast from Santa Monica to Laguna Beach, Del Mar, La Jolla, and Coronado. Soon other people came forward and wanted to put a "Happy Store" like ours in their town.

Having created the Hallmark card shops, Marv was able to structure a simple program for these people to have their own gallery. It was not a franchise, but rather a licensing arrangement, nothing too complicated. Eventually, there were twenty-six of these Sally Huss Galleries across the country with one in Japan and another in Switzerland.

Inside the La Jolla Gallery. Lots of art

Our gallery in Murten, Switzerland on the Interlochen-Oberhasli

Conveniently, the galleries, showcasing my "happy art" and writings, attracted all sorts of companies that wanted to use that art on their own products. These included lines of greeting cards for American Greetings, purses and totes, stationery, baby bibs, ceramic lines, several clothing lines, wallpaper, stitchery kits, and others products that I can't remember. All of these became available to the outlying stores to fill their racks and tables while we provided the gift art and wall art. Much of this art was created with pen and ink, that very skill I detested in grammar school!

Some of the licensed products

With the success of the galleries, we moved to La Jolla and into a beautiful, spacious, garden home, surrounded by roses, near the beach. Mike was now in high school and participating on the school tennis team. He had played some top-notch junior tennis, but his heart wasn't really in it to the degree that his mother's had been. I should have known it when in his first competitive match at seven he brought along some Legos and asked his opponent if he wanted to play with them as they changed sides.

Michael after a hit with our friend Pancho Gonzales

We did surprise Mike with a trip to Wimbledon between his junior and senior years in high school. He had been made captain of his high school team, leading them to a winning season. No easy task in Southern California. Our friend Bob Howe arranged the trip. Bob and I had been quarter-finalists in the mixed doubles division long before. Now, Bob had structured a wonderful addition to the Wimbledon experience for those past champions and near champions – The Last 8 Club. It exists today and offers those who have reached the quarterfinals or better two tickets each year to the Championships. It also allows these members to gather in their own clubhouse on the grounds where they can meet and greet old friends and competitors. Such a nice thing!

With Bob Howe on Mike's big adventure

Mike and Marv have a chat with the great champion Ken Rosewall at the Last 8 Club. The Australian won 8 Grand Slam singles titles before the Open Era.

Mike eventually went on to play for the Pac-10 Division 1 top-rated University of Arizona team under Coach Billy Wright.

The Business of Art

Filling our own stores and preparing products for the licensed stores became an enormous task. I worked fast and I worked continuously, creating new lines for the gift art baskets and new themed mono-prints and original paintings for all the stores. I did what I did without worrying about perfection. Perfection, it seemed to me, stifled people, stifled creativity. I had come across artists who worked endlessly on one painting. No, I worked on one, then moved to the next. The skill became perfected in the doing, just like tennis. Hit another ball; don't worry about the last one. The next one will surely be better. Certainly, I could see areas in a painting that I wished were a little different. On the next one I would do that. Overworking a piece of art or anything had its drawbacks – it took the life out of it. Learning to be discerning with art and everything else, without being judgmental, was a trait worth developing. Was this a conundrum? Is it possible to look at something truly objectively without judging it? To see all aspects of something, both positive and negative… that was a trick. So many prejudices, likes and dislikes, cloud our vision.

This was brought home to me in another dream. In this dream Michael Malosek, whom I held in such high regard, was walking along a beach saying, "F**k! F**k! F**k!" What was the message? Do not be judgmental. Discernment was a different matter.

I learned to make art decisions quickly and move on. I needed to work fast. The idea of creating mono-prints evolved out of a need to supply these outlying stores with large art for their customers. I couldn't stand the grayed, muddied colors that would result from a printing press that used four or six colors to generate the rest of the palette. Screen-printing was good, but expensive. Yes, you could have any color you wanted and it would be vibrant, still laying each color on a page separately was time-consuming and traditionally pricey. I could use this process and I did, for some of the art for children, by limiting the number of colors. At least the colors were bright and clean. Then, there was the mono-print. This I dreamed up out of pure necessity. It consisted of having the black line-work screen-printed on a page and then painting in the colors with real paint – bright, lively paint. This was done by hand, and not just mine. Elves helped with this process.

Painting monoprints by the dozens

It is interesting to note that during all of this hustle and bustle with art and business, I never gave a thought to where it was all going. I was simply doing it. It wasn't like there was a championship or trophy that I was trying to win. We were succeeding, for sure, yet I never looked out in front to see where this might end up. I have to attribute this lack of forward thinking to the fact that my eyes are just a little too close set, not balanced. People with eyes like mine tend to focus on detail, whereas, people with wide set eyes see the big picture. Marv's eyes are perfectly balanced and could see both. Lucky for me!

Talking with kids about art… and later, books

Nevertheless, I was not looking at an end game. Where would I ever get off of this treadmill? Ambition can be blinding. It can be a two-edged sword – useful for accomplishing; yet dangerous if not kept in check. We had the strong desire to achieve something, were determined and made the effort. Where it was going ultimately, I didn't know?

My head was focused on the next blank page or canvas. At this point, there was no slave driver other than myself. Volumes of art were created and, I have to admit, it was fun.

Looking up from my art table in my La Jolla home studio

At various times, people came forward who wanted to take over our business either by rolling out more independent stores or creating franchises. They were not necessarily people with the best intentions. Marv's wisdom in this area kept us safe from these vultures.

I also did some commission work, painting exactly what somebody wanted. Singer Jack Jones asked me to do the cover for his album honoring Tony Bennett and then another for his Christmas tunes. The head of Hillary Clinton's advance team loved my artwork and often came into the gallery in La Jolla. She spotted one of the larger gift art pieces and wanted it altered for Hillary 50th birthday present to be given to her by her team. The team members each wanted a copy too. We liked it so much that we made copies and sold them ourselves in the galleries. It was called "The Happy Child." It had a wonderful message:

A happy child makes a happy home.
A happy home promotes a happy neighborhood.
A happy neighborhood affects a city
Which in turn inspires a state.
A happy state touches a nation.
A happy nation helps create a happy world.
So, being a happy child is
The most important thing in the world!

Not being political or showing any preference, I crossed the aisle and did a beautiful oil painting of the La Valencia Hotel that Mitt Romney and his wife purchased for their home in La Jolla.

Inside the La Jolla Sally Huss Gallery

My Favorite Gallery

I'm not sure that it was my all-time favorite gallery, but the Sally Huss Gallery in La Quinta, California was just lovely.

La Quinta gallery

Perhaps I loved it because it displayed more of my fine art paintings and not just the decorative art. All the licensed products were present too – clothing, purses, greeting cards and other stationery items. I had even set up a studio area in it where I could paint while customers shopped. Then, of course, we had our tables with the gift art. People just loved those little inspirational, life thoughts, one man especially. He was the new editor of the Palm Springs newspaper – The Desert Sun. We chatted as he poked through the baskets. He told me how much he liked these positive, happy thoughts. "They might be a great addition to the newspaper," he said. Why not? "How about next to the masthead or would you prefer next to the sudoku puzzle?" Such a choice. "Of course, the masthead!" I said.

I didn't know what I was getting into. This was to be a daily panel (six days a week) with an original thought and illustration every day. This was on top of everything else I was doing. Still, I went for it.

After a few weeks in The Desert Sun with good feedback, I hooked up with a national syndicator of newspaper panels, King Features. The gig lasted twelve years, until newspapers withered with the onslaught of online news operations. I was happy to let the obligation go. I had other things to do. (They have resurfaced now o social media.)

Samples from the 3,756 newspaper panels

*

Great thoughts perpetuate themselves.

Think big!

*

We had been thinking big for a long time now. Was it time to rein it in?

25 LEARNING MORE

Returning to a Spiritual Connection

It was in the middle of all of this art activity that I reconnected with Therese. I'd been out of the spiritual loop and into raising a child, taking care of a family, and filling galleries. One day I ushered her into our gallery on the Third Street Promenade in Santa Monica. The white walls were covered with art, original paintings that sold by the bushel. I could paint simple florals or beach scenes in minutes. My helpers would frame them, hang them, and shine bright lights on them… and then sell them.

Therese was amazed at the volume of artwork and variety of products. I knew she would be curious about the writing and indeed she poked through the gift art baskets to see what I had written. It seemed to meet with her approval. Opening a thought-a-day calendar that I had done for American Greetings, she randomly glanced at the pages, and then stopped. "Here's one," she said and read it. "'Make your goals crystal clear and clearly they will become crystalized.'

This is not quite right," she said. "You must be careful. You are dealing with the truth and it must be correct."

Wise and beautiful Therese

Later I amended the verse by adding, "... provided Life doesn't have something better in mind." That satisfied her. But that was also the truth. So often we want what we want, when really, we should want what we need. Life knows best. In many of the gift art pieces I used the word "Life." I felt, it was a term everyone could understand and it wouldn't offend anyone's particular spiritual or religious affiliation. She was right, I needed to pay close attention to these thoughts I was writing; it was important that they be truthful and not just clever. There was actually a whole philosophy revealed in those pieces of gift art, and probably much of it I had learned by being in the company of the Bonis.

I kept my yellow sketchbooks close and wrote these thoughts daily. Over 300 ended up in our product line, plus the nearly 4,000 that ended up on newspapers across the country. I wrote them for myself as much for anyone else who might be reading them when I put them into product. I would just think of a theme and the words would roll out of my pen. I had forgotten about my obsession with the pen Chuck had given me and could use any available pen or pencil to record them now.

Here are just a couple of my favorites:

A day filled with joy awaits your involvement.

Life includes you in its every thought.

A person, who is like the sun, shining equally on everyone, is very great indeed.

Silence contains more than words can say.

Forget the mask. Forget the Face. Forget the skin.
Love the within – love the heart.

Focus on the positive and the rest will fall away
from lack of interest.

The days we keep are the days we are thankful for.

It was when I made contact with Therese again that I learned of the Master Omraam Mikhael Aivanhov. As I was a busy wife and mother, I only had one foot in touch with the Bonis' activities.

One afternoon, Therese brought me up to speed by telling me how she and Gianni had discovered this master and his work. Michael Malosek had passed on a few years earlier. The Bonis were still living in California and had flown to Paris on their way to Italy for some event. On their ride into the city, Gianni, a great collector of books, wanted to visit his favorite bookstore before going to their hotel. He went to the second floor of the store, but Therese was tired and stayed on the first floor. Her eye caught a brightly colored cover of a small paperback. It was one of the books from the Izvor Collection by Omraam Mikhael Aivanhov. She opened it, read the first paragraph and knew this was a master, a great master. Despite her fatigue, she ran upstairs only to find that Gianni had the very same book in his hand!

Omraam Mikhael Aivanhov at his center in France

From then on, the Bonis became acquainted with the Aivanhov books and the Master himself. They also organized a way to import the books to the U.S. so that those who were interested had access to the many books in this series already published. Naturally, The Bodhi Tree was one of the first stores that was delighted to put these books on its shelves. Aivanhov had spoken for over forty years and all of this oral teaching was recorded and put into books... now translated into thirty languages. These were books that offered practical information to help anyone live a more meaningful life.

*

We live busy lives. We live exciting lives,

But do we live meaningful lives?

*

Reading the books by Aivanhov brought me back to prioritizing the many things I was doing – what was significant and what was not.

26 A MORE MEANINGFUL LIFE

More Books, More Learning

Through the years I have gathered quite a collection of the Aivanhov books and have delved into them, sometimes continuously and sometimes sporadically. Every paragraph rings true. Each thought is something I can digest and live with. It is a philosophy that has come down through the ages and incorporates the essence of nearly every religion – brotherhood. One day we'll realize it. That will be the day when we are able to look at each other as sisters and brothers. It takes an effort to live with this vision when circumstances seem otherwise. The effort is worth it. How else are we ever going to make heaven on earth come to be? Not everyone thinks and behaves the same as everybody else. We are unequal in nearly every way. However, there is only one way in which we are equal – dignity, the dignity that comes from the fact that we are all sons and daughters of God.

Jack Canfield's Connection

At this time Marv and I continued working on art and design projects, and attending to the signature galleries around the country with all of the licensed products. However, the climate changed after 9/11 and as hard as we were working, the economy was working against us. My galleries, which were really "happy stores," began closing, one after the other.

Painting outside my last gallery in La Jolla

We were down to the last gallery in La Jolla, and I was running it myself when a friend and her husband stopped in for a visit. Jan and Ian, both motivational/inspirational speakers, took me out to dinner. Afterwards, we wandered down to the La Valencia Hotel for a little music. We were about to sit down when Jan noticed Jack Canfield and his wife Inga on the dance floor. "Come meet Jack," she said. Jack, author of the *Chicken Soup* books and more, was considered "America's Number 1 Success Coach," and Jan had worked with him for years, assisting at many of his seminars.

Jack was a warm, charismatic man in his mid-fifties

with a soft manner and an easy smile. He was someone anyone would like instantly. I really liked him.

After a bit of small talk, Jan insisted that the Canfields mosey down to my gallery for a peek. It was about ten o'clock when I opened the gallery and turned on the lights for them. Jack looked around and asked, "What do people say when they come in here?"

"That it's bright and happy." Jack shook his head in agreement.

Jan and Ian cleverly entertained Inga so that I could have some private time with Jack. He looked around some more, and then began telling me about some of his spiritual experiences. I immediately handed him the large pictorial book on Omraam Mikhael Aivanhov that I had on a side table. It had been created to mark the 100th anniversary of the Master's birth. "This is the master you need to know," I said.

Jack then sat down at the counter, and looked intensely at every picture and read every line on every page. When he seemed satisfied, he closed the book and said to the others. "We can go now. I got what I came for."

Not too long after that first encounter with Jack, my friend Jan Fraser, insisted that I attend one of his weeklong success seminars. She went to great lengths to get me there. It was being held in Scottsdale, Arizona where she had a condo in which I could stay.

A visit with Jack Canfield

Two Personal Revelations

During Jack's seminar, two interesting events occurred. The first was a special exercise. We attendees were warned that if we opened our eyes during this particular "game" we would definitely miss something. We would miss learning something about ourselves.

The room was cleared of all chairs, booklets, notepads, etc. The lights were turned off and the instruction was given to move about with our eyes closed. Naturally, everybody began bumping into each other. This was a group of two hundred and fifty people lurching about with out-stretched arms interacting with each other… but it was how each interacted that was most revealing.

Because Jack was a big believer in hugs and hugging had been a ritual during these daily sessions, hugging was the first and automatic response to encountering another attendee in this darkened room. Ah! But in my case, it was my next action that told me what I had done all my life without being aware of it. I would take one person's hand and connect it to another's. I seemed to find great satisfaction in putting people together. Connecting. I was a connector. Yes, yes, that was a truth that I had never realized consciously.

When I looked back over my past, I could see how this trait had recurred continuously in my life. If I knew something to be true, I shared it, provided someone asked. If someone needed help in the healing area, I tried to link that person to an appropriate doctor, healer, or remedy. I had studied many healing modalities and would easily pass on what I knew. I gave Gianni Boni's name to as many friends as I had, as well as Joan Englander's. If I discovered an interesting person, I had to share that person with all my friends. Once I started teaching tennis in the relaxed and powerful way that I had discovered, I was happy to pass on this information, not just to someone who might be taking a lesson from me, but to anyone I saw struggling with life. My galleries were also a place of sharing… I passed on truths in the form of those little gift art pieces. I would make these pieces of art, put them in the baskets and someone would read them… maybe it would be a particular message a person needed, a message to lighten their heart or brighten their day.

Pretty Mary Wilson with her Ralph doing a radio broadcast

Mine was a life of connecting people and information to others. Once I'd discovered how to get the man of my dreams, I gave the formula to friends. Dorothy got Michael. Joan got Bill, Ashley got George, Ann got Bob, and Mary got Ralph, then owner of the Buffalo Bills. That's what I learned in this exercise at the seminar.

At the end of the weeklong seminar with Jack, he took all of us through a wonderful meditation in which he guided us across a grassy meadow to reach the base of a spectacular mountain. On top of the mountain a beautiful, golden angel appeared holding a box. She opened the box and to each she revealed our "life purpose." Whew! Who would not want to know that?

Jack sending me off on a new adventure

When that golden angel took the lid off of the box for me, out poured my life purpose – books, books upon books, endless books. They fell in a stream down on me. I was to write books! Naturally, that's all I had secretly wanted to do, but never did. I was always trying to make enough money to give myself the time to do just that. So, I went away from this enlightening seminar, ready to start my new career.

*

Miracles fall out of the sky and into the laps

of those who expect them.

*

There is nothing like a new direction to send my heart a thumpin'.

27 A NEW CAREER

Closing Doors First

While we began transitioning our business, we began doing the same with our living arrangements. Marv had wanted to improve his golf game, so we purchased a condo at PGA West in La Quinta, California. This meant that he commuted to La Jolla on weekends, while I was still running our last little gallery there.

On a slow afternoon in the gallery on Ivanhoe, a familiar figure walked in. It was Sam. He resurfaced. I knew he had a home in the area; he loved La Jolla during the days we were together.

I was glad to see him, but still it felt a bit awkward. He seemed as warm and charming as ever and looked around the room at all the art. He seemed to approve. We chatted at the counter area for a few moments. As he spoke, he put his hands on mine with a tenderness that I remembered. When he was finished chatting, he turned and walked toward the door. Before opening it, he turned, looked back over his shoulder, and said, “I have loved three women in my life… Jennifer, Peggy, and you.” Then he opened the door and was gone. I was the only one he hadn’t married, I thought. Not a second later I heard a voice, “But you got the better man.” Yes, I got the better man – certainly the better man for me. Life knew best, as always.

When that gallery finally closed, we moved into a comfy apartment near the La Jolla Beach and Tennis Club, and were forced to let go of the condo in La Quinta.

Two unusual things happened at this point. The first was that I was driving my trusty, rusty, blue van around the corner from our apartment, on a side street, when a bicyclist flew through the air at the intersection in front of me. He had been coming down the hill and must have hit the edge of the curb. I stopped my van, hopped out expecting to see him with a broken arm or leg or something. He lay on the ground absolutely still; he was perfect, he didn’t have a mark on him. Then everything let loose and I knew he was gone. It was a disturbing image. As much as I knew about “death,” it was still unsettling. Two nights later he came to me in a “dream” and said, “Do not worry. I am fine; there was no pain.” I understood and was grateful to him for clearing my mind. Again, this was confirmation of Toddi’s explanation that there is no death, only life.

Years earlier my brother had come to me several days after passing away from a brain tumor. I had been with him in the hospital where his face had been so distorted that he was almost unrecognizable. When he visited me in a kind of “dream,” he showed me his true image… a face that was made of the most beautiful, colored lights. It was a gift to see him as he really was and to confirm my understanding that there was no separation between this world and the next.

The second unusual event that occurred during this period was that a woman came forward, intent on resurrecting my licensing business using my existing art. My heart wasn't in it, but she was wildly enthusiastic. After taking our entire inventory of products left over from our last gallery, she disappeared. It proved to be a godsend, as these things usually are. This freed me for something new – books.

Another dream clarified this new direction into books. It showed me in the passenger seat of a car that was driving on a busy highway with children lying along the sidewalk next to the car. They were in peril. In the dream, I asked, "Why isn't someone helping these children? They are in danger." No one came forward, so I got out of the car and picked up one child. I was amazed at how light he was. "Children are so easy to uplift!" I said. So, that was it: I was to uplift children by writing children's books!

Opening Another Door

With no income and no way to pay rent, we were, in a sense, homeless. Surprisingly, another friend opened a door, his door. I hadn't spoken with Jerome Gastaldi for over two years, but had an inkling to call him. He had a fabulous artist retreat/studio, called Villa Con Cuore, on the top of a hill in Fallbrook, California. It was where he painted all of the art for the Yard House Restaurants... paintings as large as a hundred feet long, square pieces of eighteen feet or twenty feet, and a multitude of smaller ones. He could teach anyone how to paint and often did. He created sculpture pieces so large that they had to be moved with a crane.

Then, there was his spiritual, inspirational artwork, mystical in nature and at the same time beautiful to the eye. He had a "hand." I mean to say, that when he painted, which he did daily, he could touch a painting with his brush and make it come to life... whether it was his painting or another's. He was truly a magical person. There was no way to define Jerome; he was one of the most exceptional people that I have ever met, full of ideas and always willing to help someone in trouble. When I explained my predicament, he invited Marv and me to settle into one of the cottages on his property.

Jerome Gastaldi preparing art for one of the Yard House restaurants

It was a divine experience... quiet, country living with an artistic atmosphere. Visitors were many and always welcomed. Jerome was so dearly loved. They were people from all kinds of backgrounds, but usually people with a spiritual base. He couldn't have been more generous. I loved being there.

Jerome with guests on the hilltop in Fallbrook

I had come to know Jerome long before when his lovely wife Anne, then single, took tennis lessons from me in Laguna Beach. While teaching her tennis, I gave her my formula for getting the man of her dreams… she got Jerome.

That was the thing about that formula. Whomever I gave it to received what they wanted – whether it was just a friend to go to dinner with or a life-long companion. For years people would pop up and tell me stories of the sweethearts they had manifested using this slam-dunk method. I finally wrote a book on it (*How to Find Your Soulmat*e.) The secret again was to be in love with the exact kind of person you wanted to have in your life before you ever met him or her. The same goes for any desire a person might have. Be there now, be at the end point emotionally from the beginning.

Who knows if I would have won Wimbledon if I had had a better understanding of the proper emotional state to play in – one of joy and confidence, fearless and trusting? Thank goodness I didn't or I may have stopped, thinking that I'd reached the ultimate goal. Instead, I found other Wimbledons to win, other mountains to climb. I still would have needed a forehand!

Look Out, Amazon!

Now, being on this property without rent to worry about, I could relax after years of intense, never-ending work and explore the opportunities presented by the e-book self-publishing craze and Amazon. Marv, being the great researcher that he was, read over a hundred books on the subject. With a few adjustments to Jerome's house, I set up a room where I could illustrate my children's books right on the computer. This was how we began our new career. I was seventy-two and Marv was eighty.

Finally, it was time for that tattered box that had traveled with me everywhere, to be brought out and the contents unloaded. Rummaging through the stories, I started picking a few, illustrating them in the simplest way and posting the files into Amazon's Kindle Direct Publishing program. I hardly knew how to turn on a computer when I started, but it didn't take me long to find a way, even a very crude way, to illustrate the stories.

We created and published book after book, all designed to uplift the lives of children by focusing on social/emotional issues and offering skills that would help a child be the best that she or he could be.

It was during this time that another dream arrived. This one was about drugs. All of the books we were creating were for children four years old to seven or eight. I knew that this was the critical period in a child's life when ideas could be planted that would positively affect that child from then on.

This was the dream: a mother is walking with her very young child, perhaps five or six years old. The child sees a large spider in its web. The spider is made of beautifully colored, glimmering jewels. It is irresistible, the child runs toward it and into the web. The child is caught.

The message was clear: drugs are like a spider's web, very attractive, alluring, but once snared and caught, it was almost impossible to get out. How to explain this lesson to a child? That's when a little mouse called Mr. Consequences showed up in my writing. Mr. Consequences' role was to help a child make good choices by understanding the consequences of bad choices. Could it be done in regards to drug use?

After months of work, we now had lots of books to tell our stories with adorable mermaids and princesses, princes, and animals of all kinds – monkeys, orangutans, koalas, turtles, rabbits, cats, dogs, and fish. There were loons, raccoons and baboons, helpful monsters, Valentine hearts, Christmas elves, and Thanksgiving turkeys. And, all the books with a dominant child character were also created with that character being tan in a multicultural version. No subject was off limits and finally even smoking, drinking, and drug use were tackled in a book with the help of Mr. Consequences.

A sample of some of the books

It has been extremely rewarding... creating these books. I still have a stack to illustrate with more inside me eager to get out.

With Marv's knees proving to be too stiff to maneuver around the hill at Jerome's, and the books providing an income, we moved once again... this time to Solana Beach, the twentieth move in our forty-year marriage.

The time in Solana Beach gave me the opportunity to not only expand our book line, but also connect with the Head Start programs in the San Diego area.

San Diego Head Start Kiddies

I had been wondering how I could get the distribution of the books beyond the usual Amazon structure. "Head Start," was what I heard, so Head Start became my focus. Through a set of coincidences, a tennis friend's husband generously underwrote the purchase of a truckload of the books for those programs.

Completing the Circle

Two years was enough in Solana Beach, the traffic was growing and we were aging. Something simpler would be appropriate, something easier. That's when we chatted with our son who was traveling through Colorado. He described the beauty, the slower pace, and the friendliness of the people. "Let's all move to Colorado," I said… and so we have.

Marv and I have planted ourselves in a little house in Colorado Springs one mile from the cottage I left forty-five years before when I came from California to be with him. Amazingly, the first person I played tennis with in the Springs when we first arrived reminded me of a piece of art that I had done for him to give to his mother on Mothers' Day long ago… and which the family still had. I never know when someone will remind me of a piece art or a special thought that I had created for them.

Now more books have been added to the catalog, including a special one for the Head Start programs in Colorado… and we just keep going! There is a wonderful book to help children understand food allergies and be tolerant and compassionate of those who have them. There is a book on juvenile diabetes and books to encourage children with these conditions to still dream big. Who knows what is next?

*

To know that your life means more

than what it means to you is well worth knowing.

*

Everyone's life means more than what they think it does. Every person interacts with others during a day. It is important that each of us remembers this and adds a little sparkle to those encounters. I have been especially lucky to be able to create art, books, and products with their own happy messages.

28 A BRIGHT FUTURE

Being Honored

I've never been much on honors or rewards… for myself that is. My rewards have been in the actual doing of something, simply enjoying the activity. As I said, we've never had a trophy case in any of our homes. However, there were a couple of special honors bestowed on me regarding my tennis accomplishments worth mentioning.

Receiving an award with Dennis Ralston

The first was a day in Bakersfield that honored both Dennis Ralston and me at our beloved Bakersfield Racquet Club. Dennis and I had grown up together on those courts and our parents had us practicing with each other before school on many mornings. Dennis was a Wimbledon champion and spent the rest of his life in the tennis arena teaching and advising young players, including Chris Evert.

Another honor given to me was being inducted into the Kern County Sports Hall of Fame. This occurred in Bakersfield and our whole family gathered for the event, plus all of my old Bakersfield Racquet Club friends, as well as Etta Gillard from the Jastro Park days. Unfortunately, it was during my days before public speaking and I simply received the award, said, "Thank you," and sat down. My nervous system was not cut out for more at that time. It was a shame because it really offered me the opportunity to thank all of the townspeople for their support through the years.

Occidental's Hall of Fame event

Fortunately, the next time I had more to say. This was an event at Occidental College in which I was inducted into Oxy's Sports Hall of Fame. It was held on a balmy evening in the town of Eagle Rock, where Occidental is located. I mixed in with the attendees and wandered among beautifully appointed dinner tables set up at the end of the football field. Everyone was dressed to the nines. I wore my favorite garb – a Buddhist Nun's golden, embroidered robe.

It was a perfect evening. Old friends had driven in from great distances for the event. My remaining family on my brother's side was there... his wife Linda, her daughter Melissa, Melissa's husband Adam and their two kids, Kenna and Cole.

The speakers before me gave long-winded speeches of old times at Oxy, the usual fare. I wanted to say something that would be helpful to those present, something they could take away with them. After I took the podium, here is what I said:

"Long ago there was an extraordinary man named Toddi, who lived in Rome and taught at the university there. He was a mathematical genius as well as a writer and humorist. Occasionally he would gather together the noted scientists in the city, who were always at odds with each other. They would study things. One time they decided to study the energies in soil. They took a box, filled it with dirt and every scientist studied it from all aspects. What they discovered was that the energies in soil were chaotic... that is, until a seed was planted. Once a seed was planted, all the energies in that soil aligned themselves to make that seed come to fruition.

That's what my father did for me... he planted the seed of a champion in me that has never stopped producing fruit. I have never stopped striving to make myself better and more useful to others. Every parent would do well to plant the seed of a champion in their children. It is not important that those children become champions in the usual sense, but only that they strive for greatness in everything they do."

I thanked the president of the college and all the other dignitaries present. When I returned to our table, I asked my sister-in-law what she thought of the speeches. She said, "I liked yours best; it was short!"

One More Hitch

It was as if we were coming out of the ashes, reinventing ourselves one more time. The little cottage we rented faced west to the Rockies. Over them I could imagine the ocean we left behind and the friends we would miss. We were in Colorado, out of the traffic and fast lane now, and we loved it.

There always seem to be more friends to discover. Tennis has continually been the perfect door-opener for me. I was introduced to a club full of tennis players, who soon became my friends. Tennis is the friendliest sport. Among them was one of the most beautiful people I have ever met and who came to be one of my dearest friends. Amanda was perfect in nearly every way, except for her forehand. I would say that purity was her essence and generosity was her nature. She took the high road whenever there was a road to take – a great role model for anyone in her presence, including me.

Amanda was well aware of our limited resources at that time and made it quite clear that whenever we went to lunch or dinner, it was on her. This she established at the beginning of our friendship because she liked to eat and enjoyed having company while she did. Also, she was hopeful I would gain a pound or two. Married to an equally outstanding person, Amanda loved her life and lived it fully.

Then, there came a time in our lives that our family's financial situation became unsustainable. Something had to be done. It was one of those circumstances that has such an unpleasant feeling to it, a hope that you don't have to deal with it. But I knew I had to.

We had been living on social security, along with drips and drabs from Amazon book sales. Marv had handled the money in our lives for years; I just earned it. When I realized the depth of our debt, I was appalled. Borrowing from Peter to pay Paul could not go on any longer. The few people to whom I divulged this dire situation, advised me to declare bankruptcy. I hardly knew what it meant. And, I hardly knew how I would approach the subject with Marv. I was in conflict over my loyalty to him and the feeling that this was something we must do. Pride was a problem; I had always honored my commitments.

There was no escape; things had to change. I did my own investigating online and determined that it was nothing I could handle myself. I needed help, a proper bankruptcy attorney. Pulling and pushing on this issue with Marv sickened me. Despite that, I continued my search. Intuition led me to a wonderful attorney who could understand my dilemma. How to step out ahead of Marv on this was my quandary. Was I brave enough, even though I felt it was the right thing to do?

I remained confused until one morning as I sat at my art table in our little cottage, a cyan blue color passed across our front window. I thought it might be our neighbor Jerry who would stop by now and then to visit Marv. I went to the door, opened it, but no one was there. It was a sign. I loved signs. Instantly, I realized that it was the same blue light that had shown up here and there in my life to guide me and give me strength. That's all the confirmation I needed to go forward with the bankruptcy. I trusted life. Now, I just had to figure out how to pay for it.

A few days before Christmas, Amanda stopped by to wish us a happy holiday. She and her husband would be going to their cabin in Aspen for a few days. I walked with her out to her car. She turned toward me, reached in her back pocket and pulled out a folded check. We looked at each other. Tears welling up in our eyes, she said, "This is just between us. Tell no one." She knew what this meant to me. A devout Christian, Amanda lived her faith every day. No more perfect a person have I ever met. Probably more perfect than Mary Poppins!

That check covered the price of the attorney and all the paperwork that went with the bankruptcy.

More Games to Play

From that moment on, we began to sail again. Marv finally came around to supporting my decision. Our son secured a job teaching tennis at the beautiful Garden of the Gods Resort on the north end of town. He had not played tennis in twenty years, not since leaving the University of Arizona. It didn't seem to matter; his strokes were intact and his enthusiasm for the game resurfaced. That contact pulled me out from behind my computer and back onto the tennis court myself to teach a bit of my Zen tennis to whomever wanted to learn to play relaxed.

Within a year I had a pickleball paddle in my hand and began teaching this game too. I saw the variety of ways you could hit a pickleball and the ease of getting newcomers into the sport, especially seniors. My tennis background was a big help, not only in my own play, but in teaching others how to move effectively and play effortlessly. Within a year, I had also written and published a simple book on the subject (*Dare to Dink*) to encourage others to put a paddle in their hand and try this activity. With fun as the goal, anyone could accomplish that no matter how well or badly they played. I found that pickleball definitely lightens hearts, tightens muscles, spreads joy, and most certainly creates a life full of new friends.

Several of those friends were encouraging, "You would do really well playing in national pickleball tournaments." The thought crossed my mind, then I heard from within, "Not on your life!" I had other things to do, I guess.

Life's Real Purpose

Long ago, I had been tempted to run off to India to seek enlightenment or to follow the latest, greatest, fashionable guru. Luckily, when I met the Bonis I knew they knew the truth on the really important matters. I always trusted that there would be some who knew what I didn't know. When I found them, I trusted them.

After studying the books of Omraam Mikhael Aivanhov, it made sense to me that the Eastern way was not my way or the best way for a Westerner. I was definitely not destined to be a yogi. And just like most everyone else, I was a regular person who had certain talents that could be used to benefit others. It also made sense to me that we are all here to do some "good" in a practical way and not escape this world into nirvana.

I saw the disasters that many had experienced from not taking care of business in their everyday lives and following a so-called spiritual leader. Long ago, during talks at the Bonis, I learned that there would be many false prophets showing up... testing our discernment, I suppose. There were and, unfortunately, probably still will be more to come. My friend Mary Ann almost lost herself by following a false Sufi. My friend Sharon nearly lost her fortune to a false mystic from India who amassed seventy-four Rolls Royces from the purses of his worshippers! How many others, hoping to find a higher purpose, were led down the garden path only to find it led to a dead end... and without any money in their pockets? What about the lost young people today, who are following the deadly path promoted by radical Islamic leaders or socialist fanatics? This search for something more to life than what appears on the surface has led our young people into the world of drugs and self-medication, each one foolishly leading the other.

Aivanhov, who was one of the twentieth century's greatest luminaries of Western spirituality, taught, among other things, about discernment, an attribute that is greatly needed at this time.

We no longer need to trek off to some ashram to be tested; the testing goes on right here in our daily lives. We can develop ourselves and improve our lives by the efforts we make and the inner work we do. I found wonderful exercises and meditations in my studies, along with concepts to be contemplated that proved their worth. Here are some: the idea of reincarnation; the importance of understanding hierarchy; the realization that as life goes on, we are working for our future NOW; and differentiating between our two natures – human and divine. I learned that our inner state is not only our private concern, but it affects all others as well. Also, I learned to appreciate the value of giving thanks at all times; the acknowledgment of a living nature; the awareness of our indebtedness to our parents, country, nature, and the Universe; and one of the most important themes – the mindfulness of how we use our energies. These are just a few examples of subjects that I have studied and worked with through the years.

As I look at this aspect of my life from a distance, it is as if I had been dropped into a vortex that few people ever get to experience. To be in the presence of such extraordinary human beings was a gift, a blessing that amazes me still. The only rationale that I can come up with as to why I found myself there is that in every arena of life that I entered, I was always seeking the best and making an effort towards it. Very simply, it might just have been the result of my eternal champion's quest.

Using What I Learned

For many years I had been creating that daily panel

for newspapers offered by King Features, as long ago predicted by Jennings Lang. They had started as an extension of my gift art line and were designed to shed a bit of light on various subjects to brighten a reader's day. Much of the philosophy housed in these little inspirational panels has come from my experiences and of being around very wise people.

One of these people, of course, was Therese. She was a great influence on my life, as she was on the lives of many others. Her presence was magnetic, charismatic, and inspiring. She filled a room just by herself. She passed away in 2013. On our last meeting, two weeks before she passed, I told her, "I will love you forever and ever," She took it in and repeated it softly, "For ever and ever." It made her smile.

Therese in her later years

Many of the themes of my children's books reveal truths that are embedded in me from the experiences I have lived through and the teachings I have been given. They are alive within me.

In writing this book, many memories have popped up, even some that I had totally forgotten or repressed. One of these, I remember now, occurred when I was six or seven and living with my family in that long, rambling, adobe house in the walnut grove of West Covina. There was a major road that ran in front of the house, a cut-through from Pasadena to the beach area. Not too many cars or trucks used this road, but when they did, they usually travelled at a fast clip. The property next to ours was an Arabian horse farm and next to that was my grammar school.

One day while walking along the edge of this road to school a truck stopped. The driver rolled down his window and asked, "Would you like a ride to school?"

"No thank you," I said. The school's entrance was just ahead. The truth was I didn't want him to go out of his way for me. I did not want to bother him. I walked on.

Recently when I told a friend about this episode, she asked, "What did you tell your mother when you got home?"

"Nothing," I said. I had not suspected any evil intent. Kids usually don't. But that could have been the end of my journey right then.

Now after all my years of twists and turns and experiences, I am eighty years old and I continue to do the work the *golden angel* revealed to me years before. I write and illustrate my children's books to my heart's content. Amazon through Kindle Direct Publishing has made it possible for me to create the many books I had dreamed of, and then made them available to a wide audience.

From the importance of having a good attitude *Positive Pete* to being appreciative *One Green Omelet, Please!* to being kind *The Monkeys Who Tried Kindness* to being cooperative *Let's Everybody Fish!* to being helpful *The Princess in my Teacup* to following your heart *The Little Leprechaun Who Loved Yellow* to valuing a mother's love *Who took my Banana?* to making good choices *No Smoking, No Drinking, No Drugs* and more, there is a lesson inside each of these books, which now number over one hundred. I feel I am one of the lucky ones who has been plucked from the depths at one time and given another chance, this time to do something worthwhile.

When I look back, I am in awe of the many people who have passed through my life, offering me ways to stay in "the light." From healers, teachers, masters, doctors, friends, family members, and strangers I have been given the gift of their presence and I am grateful. Life is wonderful! And we should never forget it.

My Sweet Sun Man

It is now fifty years since creating my Sun Letter. My Sun Man has lived up to my expectations and more.

Marv and Sally together after all these years

It doesn't mean that we have lived happily-ever-after without some bumps in the road, or some unexpected turn of events. Yet, during these learning curves and growing cycles, we have remained devoted to each other and supportive of one another. Marv's goodness, love, and strength have sustained me, and allowed me to excel in whatever mountain I wished to climb, whatever Wimbledon I wished to win. I remain forever grateful to Hallmark for caring enough to send the very best!

We still walk hand-in-hand wherever we go.

Conclusion

My life's journey is much like everyone else's, filled with ups and downs, wins and losses, surprises and disappointments. Everyone is dealt these cards; yet it is how we meet and handle them that matters. Marv and I have had one house, two houses, and been homeless. We've been successful and have had failures. We've had deaths in our family circle and births. We've had sick days and healthy ones, yet we constantly look forward to the next day. If you've got life, you've got everything that truly matters. Attitude **is** everything; be sure to pick a good one!

Being raised to be a champion has given me the tools to tackle life's challenges by emphasizing the importance of focus, effort, and discipline, while maintaining inner harmony and a positive attitude. It has made me aware of the necessity to eliminate weaknesses and at the same time appreciate what I have and have done, and what I may still accomplish. Because of this, I am grateful for the tireless efforts of others, including my family members, who have helped and guided me along my path.

When I asked my mother-in-law in her nineties what she thought she was here to do, she answered, "To be the best that I can be." That's a champion's attitude and anybody can have it at any age.

Every child can be raised to be a champion, that is, to be the best that he or she can be. If a little girl from Bakersfield can do it, so can any child.

*

Dream big, plan well, work hard, smile always,

and good things will happen.

*

Resting on my laurels

Each experience is a bead on the necklace of life. As these experiences become polished through contemplation, truths are revealed, and the beads of experience turn into pearls of wisdom, which of course can be worn on any occasion.

*****

All of Sally's books may be found on Amazon and on her website: sallyhuss.com, where some of her art is also displayed.

www.ingramcontent.com/pod-product-compliance
Lightning Source LLC
LaVergne TN
LVHW051043080426
835508LV00019B/1675

* 9 7 8 1 9 4 5 7 4 2 6 3 7 *